# UNDISCOVERED WALES

'There are certain places that are rarely ever seen;
and in those you will find a special sort of magic.'

*Nineteenth-century Indian missionary*

Kevin Walker

# UNDISCOVERED
# WALES
## FIFTEEN CIRCULAR WALKS

**F**

FRANCES LINCOLN LIMITED
PUBLISHERS

Frances Lincoln Ltd
4 Torriano Mews
Torriano Avenue
London NW5 2RZ
www.franceslincoln.com

*Undiscovered Wales*

First Frances Lincoln edition 2010

A catalogue record
for this book is
available from the
British Library

ISBN 978-0-7112-2867-2

Printed and bound in China

9 8 7 6 5 4 3 2 1

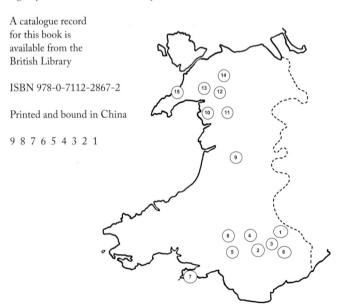

# CONTENTS

# INTRODUCTION

EVER SINCE MY CHILDHOOD I have been fascinated by man and the mountains, by the shadowy links between past lives and the more rugged places in Wales. The ruined building, the small section of once-proud masonry, the obviously man-made hole in the ground – all these pose questions which insist on an answer. No matter where I walk, even in the most 'unspoilt' countryside, there are enigmatic clues to bygone days which set my mind awondering.

During my early teens I used to attend the customary annual family holiday in Cornwall and, latterly, in South Wales. My most vivid recollections are neither of sun, sand and surf, nor of clotted cream and cornets, but of smugglers caves, tin mines, ruined castles and old wrecks. The wrecks were inaccessible, but not so the ruins, mines and caves. Such places I found irresistible, and my disobedient explorations must have driven my parents frantic with worry. Despite all sorts of dire warnings about falling down shafts and getting caught by the tide, I somehow managed to survive. So did my childhood fascination.

No regular hillwalker, rambler or mountaineer can have failed to have experienced something of this fascination, for wherever one walks off the beaten track, it is not unusual to stumble across something man-made. The lonely ruin lying in a sheltered spot miles from anywhere; the well-laid track leading from and to the middle of nowhere; the strange disturbance of landscape which is obviously man-made but whose original purpose is hidden in the mists of time. Commonly little is known about the origins of these man-made mysteries: there are few records, and those that exist are often either difficult to trace or so cryptic as to defy anything approaching a precise understanding. Despite this, or possibly because of it, such places form an integral and essential part of the landscape with which they co-exist.

Over the past thirty years I have spent literally hundreds of days tramping the Welsh mountains and moorlands, both at work and at play. I must also have spent several hundreds of hours trying to find out more about the areas through which I have tramped. I have been both delighted and appalled by the stories I have discovered, uplifted and depressed by the lives and the legends, and although there are undoubtedly thousands of sites I have yet to discover, like most outdoorsmen, I find certain areas have an enchantment which calls me back time and time again. This book is about some of those special areas – not just about landscape and scenery, but also about heritage and people, myth and legend, past lives and long forgotten tales.

Each of the routes described herein is, to my mind, a delightfully scenic walk in its own right, worthy of following even if, initially, you feel disinterested in my background ramblings (no pun intended). In any case, I firmly believe that your interest will be aroused naturally as you walk, the surroundings being such as to encourage questions from even the most ardent hater of history. I have tried to include something for everyone. Some walks pass through areas rich in legend, such as the cave where Merlin overdid his spell and unfortunately killed the person he was trying to save. Others captivate with more modern tales, like the origins of Macnamara's road, or the desperately sad story of little Tommy Jones, aged five. Several take you back to the times of lead and copper, of silver and of gold, while yet more direct you along forgotten and neglected roads to long abandoned settlements. There is often little written about these areas or their history, so while as far as is possible the stories I tell are based on fact, several rely on dubious authority and may be apocryphal. Despite what you may believe about our knowledge of the last hundred years or so, this factor applies as equally to those stories describing the more modern events as it does to the most ancient of tales.

While not one of these walks can be described as a long march of endurance, several demand a reasonable degree of stamina and a good working knowledge of mountaincraft skills (particularly navigation). Less experienced walkers are therefore asked to note the contents of the section on mountain safety. The background information preceding each walk gives, among other things, details of the distance covered, the height gained, and the type of terrain crossed, as well as noting any particular hazards which may be encountered along the route. Additionally, some of the photographs which accompany the text give a reasonable idea of what each walk entails. No matter how straightforward the ground may appear, it would be prudent to remember that inclement weather can turn the easiest outing into a potential epic, and the golden rule is to turn back if you are at all unsure. Always bear in mind the sobering fact that the landscape has, in most cases, been there for centuries (if not millennia), and will survive unscathed to be visited another day. You may not!

I have also prefaced each walk description with details of local public transport (where applicable), but it has to be said that, although rural Wales is often surprisingly well blessed in this respect, access to a car will prove invaluable. Because of this, I have chosen to describe all the walks as round trips, and each one starts from a reasonable parking area. Additionally, I have noted any amenities or facilities which will be found en route or nearby and, where appropriate, have suggested short cuts or extensions.

Although I have followed each of these walks a number of times, things do change, and I would appreciate readers' comments about any difficulties encountered when following the routes described.

Finally, may I wish you all good weather, and happy and fascinating walking.

Kevin Walker
Brecon
March 2009

# A NOTE ON MOUNTAIN SAFETY

The British weather can be fickle, nowhere more so than in the mountains, so it makes sense to be adequately prepared and equipped when following these walks – if only for your comfort! Some people seem to think that it always rains in Wales, and while this is demonstrably untrue, it is indisputable that the upland areas here are always colder, wetter and windier than the lowlands. But then, so are those elsewhere in the British Isles!

Your clothing is your first line of defence against the elements. For the upper body, it should comprise a series of layers, starting with a thin base layer designed to wick moisture away from the skin. Depending on the time of year, you will then need one or more insulating layers to keep you warm (fleeces being the best example), and it is helpful if at least one of these is reasonably wind resistant. Although it should be snug, your clothing should not restrict your movement in any way.

For the lower body, your trousers should allow free movement, and should be made from a fabric which is light, wind-resistant and quick drying. In winter or particularly cold conditions, it may be necessary to use a similar layer system to that described above. No matter what the conditions, jeans are totally unsuitable – they are usually cut too tight, and the fabric takes ages to dry out if it gets wet, providing little if any insulation. If the weather is reasonable, there is absolutely no reason that you should not wear shorts, but if you do, make sure you carry something with which to cover your legs if the need arises.

Because rain and wind will be regular companions, you will also need some form of outer shell to protect the other layers, either soft-shell or hard-shell. Arguably, if you use a soft-shell jacket, you should also carry a hard-shell jacket, although the same is not true in reverse. A good quality waterproof jacket should thus be considered an essential item of clothing, as should waterproof overtrousers. You will also need a hat (50 per cent or more of your body's heat is lost through your head), and warm gloves or mittens.

Some of these walks cross rough terrain, and I strongly recommend you wear sturdy walking boots in order to maintain good grip, to protect the feet and give support to the ankles. While some people advocate minimalist footwear, I firmly believe that you should use boots until you are experienced enough to know the limitations of your walking style and different types of footwear. As it happens, just as many foot problems are caused by bad socks as by bad boots, so treat yourself to a decent pair of socks, and consider wearing thin liner socks as well. Gaiters are not required unless you are following the routes in very wet (or winter) conditions.

Although I have tried to describe the routes in a way that makes them simple to follow, you will still need to carry the relevant map and a compass . . . and know how to use them! For the most part, route finding should be reasonably straightforward on a day with good visibility – but it could well be a different proposition if the mist descends, particularly in the wilder areas. Unless your map is laminated, you will also need a waterproof map case. A GPS device, while completely unnecessary, might give you useful information which would otherwise be difficult to obtain. It will not, however, solve any navigation problems for you.

You will need plenty to drink and something to eat, plus a little extra in reserve in case you are unexpectedly delayed. Your food should be nutritious, with a fairly high calorific value – after all, you will be using a fair amount of energy. To complete your 'hill kit', you should carry a basic first aid kit, and everyone in the party should have a survival bag (*not* a foil blanket), a head torch (with a good battery), and a whistle (to be used *only* to call for help). You will also need a small day sack in which to carry all your stuff.

In the event of an accident or injury, get the casualty into the survival bag, insulate them from the ground, and give reassurance – a little TLC goes a long way. Signal your distress or – if you have a mobile phone and reception – call 999, ask for police, then ask for mountain rescue. The International Mountain Distress Signal is six blasts on the whistle (or six flashes of a torch), followed by a minute's silence, repeated until help arrives. The answer is three blasts (three flashes), followed by a minute's silence, repeated until contact is made.

In winter conditions when there is snow and ice on the ground, some of these walks become serious undertakings. It is a sobering fact that the vast majority of winter accidents are initiated by simple slips on easy terrain. Bearing that in mind, you should not venture on to snow-covered hills without an ice axe – and the skill to use it! You will also need to take extra clothing and food, and because winter days are short, a good head torch should be considered an absolute essential.

Two final points are worth noting. First, get a good *local* weather forecast before you go. Special mountain forecasts are available for the Brecon Beacons and Snowdonia, and the Met Office provide excellent local forecasts for various regions of Wales on their website. Don't be afraid to change your plans or delay your outing if the weather looks unpromising – you will enjoy the walk even more if you leave it until a good day.

Second, always leave word of where you are going (and what time you aim to be back) with someone reliable, and just as important, let them know when you have returned safely. In the event that you do not return, the alarm can be raised promptly, and the search team will have an idea of what you were planning to do, which should help them find you.

This is not a book about safety or mountaincraft skills, and the foregoing advice is purely a brief summary. If you wish to learn more about such things, can I draw your attention to two of my previous books, *The Essential Hillwalkers Guide*, and *Navigation: Finding Your Way on Mountain and Moorland*, both of which are also published by Frances Lincoln.

Some of the walks in this book travel through terrain which is potentially dangerous. While every care has been taken to describe the routes in sufficient detail and to emphasise any hazards, things change over time, and every person choosing to follow these walks will need to exercise a degree of caution and common sense. Neither the author nor the publisher can be held liable for any losses or injuries, physical or otherwise, sustained while following or attempting to follow the walks described herein.

## Maps

The sketch maps in this book are meant solely as a guide, and not as an alternative to the appropriate Ordnance Survey or Harvey map. Only those features considered particularly relevant to each walk are shown, and all scales are approximate. The maps are loosely based on out-of-copyright Ordnance Survey mapping, amended by eye and GPS information.

## Key

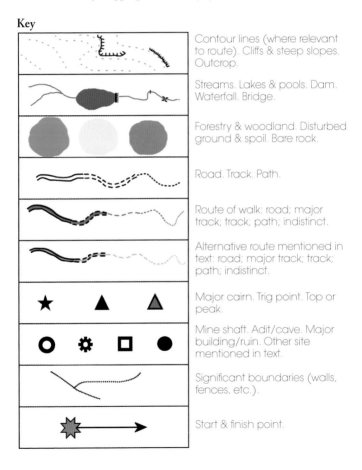

Contour lines (where relevant to route). Cliffs & steep slopes. Outcrop.

Streams. Lakes & pools. Dam. Waterfall. Bridge.

Forestry & woodland. Disturbed ground & spoil. Bare rock.

Road. Track. Path.

Route of walk: road; major track; track; path; indistinct.

Alternative route mentioned in text: road; major track; track; path; indistinct.

Major cairn. Trig point. Top or peak.

Mine shaft. Adit/cave. Major building/ruin. Other site mentioned in text.

Significant boundaries (walls, fences, etc.).

Start & finish point.

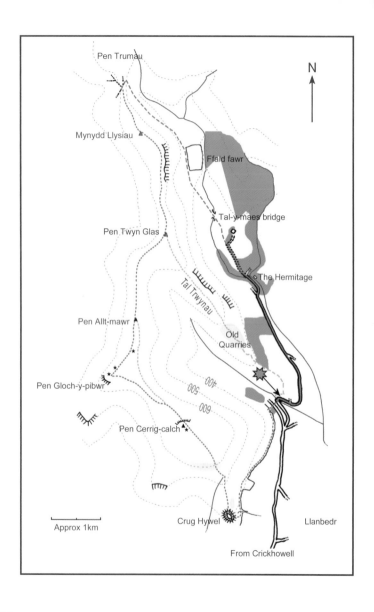

N

Pen Trumau

Mynydd Llysiau

Ffald fawr

Tal-y-maes bridge

Pen Twyn Glas

The Hermitage

Tal Trwynau

Pen Allt-mawr

Old Quarries

Pen Gloch-y-pibwr

400
500
600

Pen Cerrig-calch

Approx 1km

Crug Hywel

Llanbedr

From Crickhowell

# 1.
# MACNAMARA'S ROAD
# & THE CEFN-FFORDD

A long but mostly gentle walk, starting through a lonely valley on an old road with a surprising history, returning on an ancient track along the top of one of the fantastic 'never-ending ridges' of the Black Mountains, complete with ancient boundary stones, Bronze Age burial cairns, ghost stories, and an Iron Age hill fort of vital strategic importance!

## BACKGROUND INFORMATION

**Location** In the Black Mountains, near Crickhowell, a village situated on the main A40 between Abergavenny and Brecon.

**Start & finish point** Rough lay-by/car park at SO234229, at the hairpin bend on the minor road running north from Crickhowell, past Llanbedr, to The Hermitage.

**Maps needed** OS Explorer OL13.

**Map distance** 20 kilometres.

**Height gain** 600 metres.

> The route can be shortened to 15 kilometres with 450 metres of ascent by following the escape route from Pen Twyn Glas.

**Terrain** Excellent paths for the most part, although the section along the ridge can be muddy after wet weather, and the climb on to Pen Allt-mawr is loose and some may find it daunting. The path across the Allt-mawr plateau is awkwardly bouldery in places.

**Duration** Allow 6 hours.

**Hazards** No specific hazards, but the ridge lies at an elevation of between 600 and 700 metres above sea level and offers very little in the way of natural shelter. Standard mountain safety advice applies.

**Public transport** There is a reasonable bus service along the A40 between Abergavenny and Brecon. The nearest railway station is at Abergavenny.

**Amenities/facilities** Crickhowell is a bustling village with a good selection of shops and an inordinate number of excellent hostelries and guesthouses. There are two banks (Lloyds TSB & NatWest) and a post office.

THE OLDER I GET, the more I become convinced that I am a late developer. I keep on finding new places, new gems, often in areas I have neglected because I felt, in earlier years, that they did not have much to offer in the way of interest. For example, it was not that long ago that I thought that walking in the Black Mountains, though good exercise and pleasantly scenic, was nothing to write home about. I failed to appreciate the grand architecture – the broad, rounded tops separating wide, tranquil valleys; the uniquely stepped slopes, alternating between gentle and imposingly steep. It was only comparatively recently that I began to value the wonderfully relaxed feeling of freedom you get from striding out along these warmly mysterious, never-ending ancient ridges.

There is no better centre for walking in this area than Crickhowell, a bustling village with a stunning multi-arched stone bridge across the River Usk and a history stretching back to way before the time of the Marcher Lords. A recent marketing brochure described the place as the 'Centre of the Universe', and I have a considerable degree of sympathy with this viewpoint. Crickhowell does have that certain something.

To be frank, I have to admit to a degree of bias, for I am an ex-resident of Crickhowell and have run part of my business from the village for the past thirty years. Although I now live in Brecon, some 12 miles away, I still meet many of my clients at the famous (some would say infamous) Bear Hotel, the centre of village life, and I would have huge difficulty in finding an alternative venue of similar quality and atmosphere. But while the place undoubtedly had a profound influence on me, my residence there also resulted in my becoming blasé about some of the local hills. I am convinced it is a truism that we never really appreciate what is on our back doorstep, and the Black Mountains were not just on my doorstep, but virtually in my back garden for almost a decade. As is so often the case, it was not until I moved to Brecon that these rounded ridges began to work their magic.

Overlooking, some might say dominating, Crickhowell from the north, is a large, sloping, flat-topped hummock known locally as Table Mountain, sitting solidly on a spur which has spawned from the boulders, bracken and bulk of Pen Cerrig-calch, one of the southernmost prominences of the Black Mountains. The hummock is an important archaeological site, responsible for Crickhowell's very existence, for on and around its summit are the remains of an Iron Age hill fort, Crug Hywel, one of the earliest settlements in the area and certainly the most impressively situated. Over the years after the Roman invasion, the people from this settlement moved down into the valley, soon nestling around the security of a Norman castle, which was built at the crossing point of the river. Being on one of the major east–west lines of communication through Wales (the London to Carmarthen coach road ran this way), the settlement flourished, and as English merchants and entrepreneurs moved in, so *Crug Hywel* became anglicised to Crickhowell . . . of which, more later.

While a trip up Table Mountain direct from Crickhowell is a pleasant enough stroll for a summer's afternoon, it is far more atmospheric to approach it from the north. This has the added advantage of increasing both the scenic and heritage interest of the walk. For a start, there's the lonely Grwyne Fechan valley, full of strange tales and intrigue, then it's up on to the ridge with soaring buzzards and the occasional red kite, along an ancient trackway past old boundary stones, and up again on to a marvellous plateau where the Bronze Age people buried their heroes overlooking the wooded valleys below. The final approach to Crug Hywel is thus made along what was probably the original road, a Cefn-ffordd or Ridgeway, and gives a panoramic and strangely atmospheric view of what must once have been a major settlement.

The walk itself starts inauspiciously at a muddy lay-by on the far side of a hairpin bend and small bridge, most easily reached along the increasingly narrow lane which starts as a residential street to the west of the Shell petrol station in Crickhowell. Leaving the confines of your car at the lay-by, continue along the quiet lane for about 2 kilometres to reach a gate (sometimes closed and padlocked) where a sign informs you that the road is private and no vehicles are allowed beyond this point. Just past this sign, half hidden among the trees on the opposite side of the brook, lie the sparse ruins of The Hermitage, and the start of a story which continues for the next 10 kilometres or so.

Legend has it that in the late eighteenth century, there lived in Llangoed Castle, north of Brecon, a man of dubious reputation by the name of John Macnamara. The squire of the huge Llangoed Estate in the Wye Valley, he owned vast tracts of land in and to the west of the Black

Mountains. He was not, however, what one could call a model member of society. He drank, gambled, and womanised, was a founder member of the notorious Hellfire Club, and bled the estate towards ruin. According to local tales, it was John Macnamara who had The Hermitage built as a comfortable love nest for himself and his many mistresses.

Llangoed Castle, an exclusive hotel once owned by the late Sir Bernard Ashley (Laura Ashley's husband), is situated near the village of Llyswen, in the Wye Valley north of Brecon. The most direct route to The Hermitage is thus blocked by the westernmost ridge of the Black Mountains, so John Macnamara ordered the building of a road which would allow him to travel in his coach and pair over the mountain ridge and down the Grwyne Fechan valley, thus approaching his love nest from the north. A not-inconsiderable feat of engineering for its time, much of this road still exists. Indeed, you are about to follow it through the valley.

Continue along the tarmac past The Hermitage, soon crossing the Hermitage Bridge, beyond which you bear left up a rough track, eventually leaving the trees behind and starting to get a better view of the valley through which you are travelling. Just beyond the brow of the hill, at the next, narrow band of conifers, go straight ahead through a gate on to a grassy track, soon coming to a second gate from where the track descends into the valley and crosses a beautiful old stone bridge – Tal-y-maes Bridge. The line of Macnamara's Road is now obvious, travelling across the western slopes of the stunning and increasingly wild Grwyne Fechan valley, soon running alongside a large, stone-walled sheepfold (Ffald Fawr – which, literally translated, means 'big sheepfold'!). Just beyond this, the track curves left around a slight spur and the head of the valley comes into view. Despite regular use by countless pony trekkers, the road is still in a remarkably good state of repair along this section, and much of the original buttressing is intact.

At the far end of the valley the track deteriorates and makes a sharp left turn as it swings towards the saddle above. It is at this bend that the story resumes, for it was here, according to tradition, that John Macnamara met his death in 1818. Apparently, or so the story would have us believe, after a particularly debauched and drunken session at The Hermitage, he challenged a colleague to a race. The bet was that he would be the first to reach Tretower, a superb fortified manor house and associated hamlet,

*The valley of the Grwyne Fechan, with Tal-y-maes Bridge and the line of Macnamara's Road obvious along the left side.*

which lies in the Rhiangol Valley to the west. John Macnamara was to travel along his road in his coach and pair, while his colleague was to travel on horseback along the coach road from Crickhowell. It was an uneven contest. Not only did John Macnamara lose his bet, he also lost his life, for his coach overturned going around the bend at breakneck speed and he was thrown out and killed. But that was far from the end of the story, as you will shortly see.

The view from the saddle is breath-taking, and in complete contrast to the confines of the wild valley through which you have been travelling for the past hour or so. As you reach the top, the twin humps of the Brecon Beacons come into view, standing proud on the far horizon, and the green patchwork of the Rhiangol Valley appears at your feet. Ahead and slightly right, the bulky, rounded summits of Mynydd Troed and Mynydd Llangors obstruct the view of Llangorse Lake, while further to the right the view opens out as you look towards Llangoed Castle and the wide valley of the Wye. Macnamara's Road continues down into the valley, heading towards Cwmdu and Tretower, but here you must leave

*Talymaes Bridge – built to carry Macnamara's Road over the Grwyne Fechan stream.*

it, turning instead to the left and following the path which makes it way along the centre of the ridge, climbing shortly to a small and unimpressive pile of stones which marks the summit of Mynydd Llysiau.

Continue in a southerly direction along the ridge-top path, with panoramic views. The route you are following is ancient, a *cefn-ffordd*, possibly one of the earliest lines of communication in the area. I have heard it referred to locally as the Cefn-ffordd Ridgeway – a good example of 'Wenglish', as *cefn-ffordd* literally means, 'ridge-way'! Despite the questionable nomenclature, the route has an ancient feel and would have provided relatively safe passage for people moving between the various settlements. Travelling along ridges was much safer than journeying through the valleys which, in ancient times, were heavily wooded and full of a large number of nasty creatures such as wolves, bears and hyenas, not to mention unfriendly natives. The ridge seems endless, but offers gloriously easy walking as it heads towards the obvious hump of Pen Allt-mawr, some 5 kilometres away.

About a kilometre before the low, rounded summit of Pen Twyn Glas, on top of a small rise, lie two inscribed boundary stones, their inscriptions all but erased by two hundred years of exposure to Welsh mountain weather. If you look carefully, you will see that one is marked 'Tretower', while the other has a large carved 'M'. This is where we rejoin the story of John Macnamara, for the 'M' refers not to him, but to his wife, and as you continue along the ridge on to Pen Twyn Glas itself, you will pass several more stones, some bearing her full name.

*The Grwyne Fechan valley from Mynydd Llysiau. The heavy frost has made the line of Macnamara's Road obvious.*

These stones mark the boundary of the Llangoed Estate, as it was when John Macnamara died. How he came by the estate is an important part of the story, for he is supposed to have won it in a card game with a Mr Williams of Old Gwernyfed. Moreover, he is alleged to have promised that he would sell the estate back to Mr Williams or his descendents when he was 'no longer on the land'. On his death, therefore, several local landowners (including Mr Williams) rubbed their hands with glee as they supposed that his wife would sell up and move away – after all, in those days, women did not run large estates. However, such feelings were short-lived as Mrs Macnamara proved to be a formidable businesswoman. Not only did she take over the running of the estate, much to the horror of the local gentry, but she also had her husband laid to rest in a specially constructed stone vault, built above the ground in a newly consecrated cemetery near Llangoed, so that he would remain 'on the land until Judgement Day'. To emphasise her determination to maintain ownership of the estate, she also had boundary stones erected as a visible indicator of the extent of her land in the Black Mountains. A plucky lady!

*The summit of Pen Allt-mawr.*

There is an interesting escape route from Pen Twyn Glas, useful if the weather is threatening or you feel like an early pint, for by bearing left and heading south-east, a well-defined if grassy path leads you gently down the Tal Trwynau spur and into an area of obviously disturbed ground. These shallow pits are the remains of extensive tile stone quarries which date back to the 1700s, the rock hereabouts splitting naturally and easily into slabs which were used for building materials, and particularly for flagstones and roofing tiles. The rock was dug by hand using picks and crowbars, and then carried down into the valley on wooden sledges pulled by ponies.

The path through the quarries becomes better defined the further you descend, eventually becoming a good track which drops steeply alongside a conifer plantation. At the bottom of the field below, bear right on to the continuation of the track which descends between stone walls. After a couple of hundred metres you come to a waymarked stile on the right, beyond which a faint but waymarked path heads steeply down a grassy field. Turn left at the bottom to return to the parking area. Please keep to the waymarked path if you decide to follow this route, as this is an area in which there is one of those protracted access disputes.

Back on the ridge at Pen Twyn Glas, the main route bears right and continues along a well-defined path which heads in a westerly direction, soon curving left towards the darkly looming bulk of Pen Allt-mawr. Do

*Retrospective view of the Allt-mawr plateau, with Pen Allt-mawr on the right, and Pen Gloch-y-pibwr on the left.*

not be too down-heartened! The final ascent, though steep and loose, is relatively painless if taken steadily, and the worst can be bypassed if necessary by taking a flanking path to the right (although you will lose much of the atmosphere!). The reward for your efforts? A stunning panoramic viewpoint – arguably the best in the Black Mountains – extensive through 360°. And if it is breezy, there is a welcome dry-stone shelter next to the trig point where you can escape from the wind for a few moments – a good place to break open the thermos (or light the primus) and relish that delightful feeling of being at the top!

The next objective is Pen Cerrig-calch, the shallow dome lying just east of south, at the far end of the obvious curving plateau. You have a choice of routes. You can either approach it directly by following the well-defined if sometimes awkwardly stony path that hugs the left (eastern) edge of the plateau, or you can extend the walk by a mere couple of hundred metres and follow a slightly more panoramic path along the right (western) edge of the plateau to Pen Gloch-y-pibwr, another fine viewpoint, eventually approaching Pen Cerrig-calch from the west. There are several early Bronze Age cairns along this latter route. Whichever route you choose, look out for the ghosts! There are numerous local stories about people having strange encounters on the Allt-mawr plateau, the most common involving an elderly couple, dressed in Victorian clothing, who appear as if from nowhere, and then disappear just as quickly. They are always walking along the path, but are never close enough for any form of conversation. Despite much research, I have been unable to find out anything more about this mysterious pair.

The summit of Pen Cerrig-calch is guarded by a low outcrop of limestone, beyond which is a large Bronze Age cairn and another trig point. The onward route is not particularly well defined, and is therefore potentially confusing, particularly in poor visibility, but as long as you head roughly south-east, you will not go far wrong (in good visibility, head straight towards the summit of Sugar Loaf, standing proud in the distance). In any event, the path soon becomes better defined, skirting along the right side of a peaty boulder field – the result of a furious peat fire that burned here for weeks in the mid-1980s. This fire was quite spectacular when viewed from the mountain opposite, for the top of Pen Cerrig-calch glowed like a volcano and the plume of smoke could be seen for miles. For several years afterwards, the limestone boulders thus exposed and bleached shone white in the sunshine, to the extent that in summer it looked as though the mountain had a snow cap! The rocks have weathered now and lost much of their whiteness, but the effect can still be seen on particularly sunny days.

Continuing down an awkwardly rocky section, the Iron Age hill fort of Crug Hywel soon emerges beyond the convex slope ahead, and the path soon eases on to peaty turf and trends towards the south past springs and old, shallow quarries. Eventually you reach a Y-junction where you should take the right-hand branch, which quickly becomes rockier and curves down the front of the short, steep spur of Trwyn Ysgwrfa, at the base of which are several springs. The onward route is obvious along the centre of the ridge below, and leads straight to the northern ramparts of Crug Hywel.

The hill fort of Crug Hywel is set in a commanding position and must have been an important and powerful settlement – try to imagine what it must have been like to attack it as you climb on to its strangely flat yet sloping summit! To be technical, it is a bivallate enclosure with an inner rampart that appears to have been stone walled, with six, roughly circular building platforms. Crug Hywel means Hywel's Fort, and according to local legend, the Hywel in question was Hywel Dda, also known as Hywel the Good – one of the most important people of early Welsh history. The grandson of Rhodri Mawr (Rhodri the Great), Hywel Dda was born towards the end of the ninth century, and by about AD 942 he had claimed the title 'King of All Wales'. He is also credited with creating Wales' first formal legal system, a unifying force in an often troubled land, and one that remained intact until the Act of Union with England in 1536. However, although this is an imposing hillfort and is obviously an important site that may well have been used by Hywel Dda, the fortress itself predates him by over a thousand years, and its origins are lost in the mists of time. Additionally, and despite what many of the locals might tell you, it is now generally accepted in scholarly circles that the Hywel

*Approaching Crug Hywel (Table Mountain).*

referred to is not Hywel Dda after all, but Hywel ap Rhys of Morgannwg, who lived around the same time (AD *c*.830–86).

Having explored the site, leave the hill fort via the original gateway (the obvious cutting through the ramparts on the eastern side), and follow any of several paths leading down and left towards the farmland below, with great views of the western slopes of the Sugar Loaf (Mynydd Pen y Fal). Half way down, look for a solitary tree growing from a low outcrop to your left. If you detour along the path beneath this tree and are brave enough to negotiate the muddy section, you will soon reach a marvellous spring which may well have been the water supply for the hill fort. The water is ice-cold and sweet – a refreshing tonic towards the end of a long, hot summer's day. I have drunk from it on many occasions without ill-effect.

On reaching the stone wall separating the farmland from the open hillside, turn left and follow a reasonable path above the fields, mostly alongside the wall, for almost 2 kilometres, until you come to a small wood, at the end of which there is a waymarked stile on the right which gives access to a path that is currently not shown on OS maps. Follow this path down the left side of the wood, across a lane, and down another field, at the bottom of which it conveniently emerges by the bridge and hairpin bend, just beyond which you parked your car.

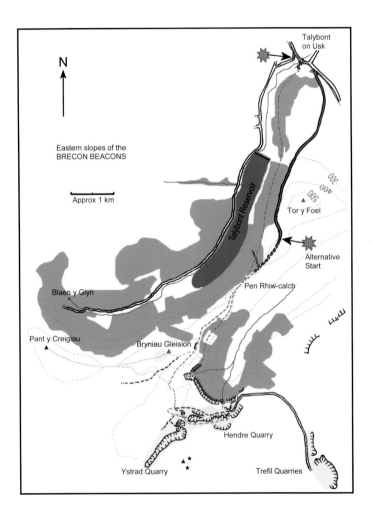

N

Talybont
on Usk

Eastern slopes of the
BRECON BEACONS

Approx 1 km

Talybont Reservoir

Tor y Foel

400
300

Alternative
Start

Blaen y Glyn

Pen Rhiw-calch

Pant y Creigiau

Bryniau Gleision

Hendre Quarry

Ystrad Quarry

Trefil Quarries

# 2.
# TRAMROADS AND GREEN LANES

An atmospheric walk on the edge of the central Brecon Beacons, crossing the cultural divide between mid- and South Wales along an old tramroad linking the canal at Talybont on Usk to once important quarries near Trefil. The return journey involves a short stretch of cross-country walking followed by a scenic saunter along an ancient track. There are several alternative routes allowing you to make the walk shorter or longer – all of which are mentioned in the text.

## BACKGROUND INFORMATION

**Location** In the eastern Brecon Beacons, at Talybont-on-Usk, easily reached from the A40 through the Usk Valley between Brecon and Abergavenny.

**Start & finish point** Rough lay-by/car park at SO112227, on the far (southern) side of the drawbridge across the canal in Talybont-on-Usk. Alternatively, to shorten the route, use the rough parking area at SO109188, at the far end of the (very) narrow and (fairly) steep lane that leaves across the canal at the eastern outskirts of the village (just to the west of the Travellers Rest Inn).

**Maps needed** Unfortunately, this walk is right on the split between both OS Explorer OL12 & OL13; and OS Landranger 160 & 161, which is rather inconvenient, to say the least. However, the entire walk is covered by Harvey Superwalker – Brecon Beacons East, and the shorter walk is just covered by OS Explorer OL12.

**Map distance** 21 kilometres.

**Height gain** 500 metres.

This can be reduced to 13 kilometres with a height gain of just 150 metres by using the alternative starting point mentioned above. It can also be extended by 7 kilometres (with an extra 100 metres of ascent) by adding the Pant y Creigiau loop, described later.

**Terrain** Excellent paths for the most part, although the section around the head of Dyffryn Crawnon can be tricky and should be approached with care. Short sections can be extremely muddy, particularly on the tramroad approaching the head of Cwm Crawnon, the cross-country section between the quarries and the ancient track, and along the Pant y Creigiau ridge.

**Duration** Allow 6 hours for the full route, and 3½ hours for the shorter route. Allow an additional 1½ hours for the Pant y Creigiau loop.

**Hazards** Steep drops from a rough path around the head of Cwm Crawnon. Loose rock, sudden vertical faces and slurry pits in the quarries. In misty conditions, navigating the Pant y Creigiau loop and the section between the quarries and the ancient track demands a modicum of skill. After very wet weather, a short section of the ancient track can become flooded.

**Public transport** There is a reasonable bus service to Talybont-on-Usk from Abergavenny and Brecon. The nearest railway stations are at Abergavenny and Merthyr Tydfil.

**Amenities/facilities** Talybont-on-Usk has a village store and several pubs, one of which (The Star) is renowned for its real ales.

THE THING THAT FASCINATES ME about this route is the contrast ... I must have walked it dozens of times over the years, yet it has never failed both to shock and to please. Perhaps part of its unique character is that it can elicit such extremes of emotion. For example, while some of the walk is enchantingly tranquil, the section around the old quarries has a brooding, melancholic atmosphere that adds a totally different dimension. Indeed, the journey through this middle section can be a surreal experience, particularly in misty conditions. It is not an area that you will forget in a hurry!

The walk starts and finishes at Talybont-on-Usk, a small, friendly village which won the Powys 'Village of the Year Award' in 2003. A thriving farming and tourist centre, its history is inextricably linked with that of both the Brecon & Abergavenny Canal and the Brinore Tramroad, and – perhaps more surprisingly – with the limestone, coal and iron industries of the South Wales Valleys. You will get to understand many of these links as you follow the walk, but a little background will not go amiss.

Construction of the Brecon (or Brecknock) & Abergavenny Canal started in 1797, and the complete route was officially opened in 1812. Considered by many to be the most beautiful canal in Britain (with some justification), it follows the Usk Valley between Brecon and Pontypool, and either lies within, or forms the boundary of, the Brecon Beacons National Park for its entire length of 53 kilometres. Although commonly regarded as a feature in its own right, it is difficult to over-emphasise the importance of its connections with an extremely complex network of tramroads (of which the Brinore was but one), and with the Monmouthshire Canal, with which it merged near Pontypool. Indeed the importance of this latter connection is well illustrated by the fact that the canal is nowadays more commonly called the Monmouthshire & Brecon Canal.

The canal is unique in that it is the only one in Britain built mainly for agricultural purposes. Whereas most other canals were constructed to transport iron and coal to the coast, the vast majority of the cargoes carried here comprised farm produce, manure, lime and basic slag fertiliser, these being transported in horse-drawn barges. Admittedly, some coal was carried, a proportion of which would have been used to fuel some of the many limekilns built alongside the canal, but most was destined for domestic use. While many British canals began to go into decline from about the 1830s, the Brecon & Abergavenny canal held on for some time, the last commercial traffic to pay tolls being as late as 1933. Restoration work began in 1968, since when the canal has gained a new lease of life, and it is now is a popular and busy attraction. Interestingly, the restoration actually began at Talybont on Usk, for the original wooden drawbridge across the canal had been replaced in the 1940s by a fixed bridge with a clearance of just 0.6 metres, effectively cutting the canal in two. The first job, therefore, was to replace this with the steel drawbridge you see today.

The Brinore (or Bryn Oer) Tramroad was built around 1815 by George Overton, who not only constructed the Penydarren Tramroad near Merthyr Tydfil (on which Richard Trevithick's locomotive ran) but also the Stockton & Darlington Railway, generally considered to be the first railway – although predated by the Brinore Tramroad by ten years. For those of you interested in the technical stuff, the tramroad had a gauge of 3 feet 4 inches (just over 1 metre) and comprised sections of L-shaped cast-iron rails held in place by combined tie-bars and chairs (known as sills), resting on stone sleepers. It was built to link the extensive limestone quarries around Trefil and important coal mines at Bryn Oer (between Tredegar and Rhymney), to the canal at Talybont-on-Usk, thus giving access to what were seen as lucrative markets in the Usk Valley and beyond. A large battery of limekilns was built alongside the

*The Brecon & Abergavenny Canal at Talybont on Usk.*

canal at Talybont, and these used the limestone and coal carried along the tramroad to produce lime, which was then transported along the canal to farms and markets at places such as Brecon, Hay on Wye, and Abergavenny. Things continued with little change until the mid-1850s, when Trefil quarries started to go into decline. Additionally, as railways began to be developed more widely, the need for the tramroad declined even further, and it had fallen into disuse by the 1870s. A rather short life for so influential an industrial feature.

The walk itself begins quietly enough along an interesting section of the canal. From the parking area, cross the steel drawbridge, and follow the towpath to the right, walking alongside but above the main village street on a high embankment. You soon reach an aqueduct over the Caerfanell stream where, on the far side of the canal, there is an overflow weir designed to prevent the water in the canal from rising to dangerous levels. Despite this safety system, on 8 December 1994, after a period of torrential rain, part of the embankment above the main street collapsed allowing an estimated 2.5 million litres of water and hundreds of tonnes of mud and stones to cascade into the village, devastating nineteen properties including fifteen houses and The Star Inn (an award-winning CAMRA pub where the beer cellar literally filled roof-full with thick, glutinous mud). It took British Waterways four months to repair the canal (and empty and clean the cellar), but there is now little sign of the devastation – apart from a display of fascinating photographs in The Star Inn. I mention this as it provides an excellent excuse for a welcome pint at the end of the walk!

Shortly after the aqueduct, leave the canal at the first bridge, cross it, and continue straight on along a tarmac lane, climbing gently and ignoring two turnings to the left. There are several signposts here – follow the ones directing you to the Brinore Tramroad. The lane soon deteriorates and curves around to the left, crossing a bridge, high above the course of the Brecon & Merthyr Tydfil Junction Railway. This railway was built in 1863, thus post-dating the Brinore Tramroad by almost fifty years, and was a busy line until closed during the Beeching purge of 1962, although the southern end now has a new lease of life as it carries the Brecon Mountain Railway, a popular tourist attraction. Turn right on the far side of the bridge, and the Brinore Tramroad stretches out in front of you.

The line of the tramroad is obvious for the next 5 kilometres – fairly straight and always heading uphill at the same gentle rate. Follow the signs (wooden finger-posts bearing the imprint of a tramcart wheel), shortly entering a more wooded section where there are many stone sleepers bearing the marks of the sills, and an excellent information board erected by the Brinore Tramroad Conservation Forum. At the next junction, the temptation will be to veer off to the right, but you need to keep straight on along what initially appears to be a much narrower path. This soon widens again, and after a slightly more rocky section, your eyes will be drawn to the right where you get superb views of the eastern slopes of the Brecon Beacons and, nearer at hand, the Talybont Reservoir Dam.

The Talybont Reservoir supplies water to Newport via a 50-kilometre pipeline. Originally proposed in 1917, there were numerous difficulties in getting the scheme off the ground, and it was not fully realised until the late 1930s. The surrounding forestry was planted as a means of using the suddenly defunct upland pastures of the twenty-five farms that were flooded, which explains some of the seemingly random ruined walls and remnant hedges. After particularly dry periods, when the level of the water drops, the ruins of one of the farms appears on an island towards the far side of the reservoir – a physical reminder of a bygone age.

Just after a second gate (roughly opposite the dam), the tramroad bears slightly left and becomes narrower and slightly overgrown, but still easy and obvious. Much of the forestry in this area has been clear-felled, so the further you go, the more extensive the views. Inevitably, however, you soon plunge back into the sterile gloom of a conifer plantation. To your left is a closely planted section where there is nothing but dead needles on the ground – no undergrowth, no young trees, little in the way of wildlife. To your right, the planting is slightly more open and is interspersed with the occasional deciduous tree. As a result, there is more in the way of undergrowth and wildlife. In the middle of this wooded section are the remains of a 'turnout' – a short section of double track where trams could

*The Brinore Tramroad approaching Pen Rhiw-calch.*

pass each other. This is reasonably obvious, not only because of the slight widening of the path, but also because the track at the turnouts was secured directly to the sleepers with wrought-iron spikes, so keep your eyes open for sleeper stones with holes drilled into them.

Shortly after this wooded section, a modern graded forestry track comes in from the right. Ignore it. Go straight across and rejoin the tramroad on the far side, now far more overgrown. Soon, once again, you're out of the woods and into a clear-felled area – keep straight on along the obvious path with its stone sleepers, ignoring a path to the right, with great views across Glyn Collwn and back towards Tor y Foel. Eventually you catch up with the forestry again (but only on the right) along a section with perhaps the best preserved stone sleepers so far.

Soon after the next gate, a stony track comes in from the right, crosses, and heads up hill to the left. As before, ignore this, continuing straight ahead along the tramroad as it follows a wide shelf cut into the hillside. At the next junction, a muddy track crosses from left to right and disappears downhill. Continue straight ahead into a cutting until the way is blocked by a steep bank, then climb to the right to reach a rough lane where there is a finger post and large stone sign. This is Pen Rhiw-calch, where a fine stone bridge once carried the lane across the tramroad. Sadly, it was demolished in the 1960s, the rubble being used to fill the cutting. The nearby scant ruin is believed to be that of the Rock Inn, one of three ale houses used by the tramroad drivers. The views here are stunning.

To shorten the walk, drive to a rough parking area at SO109188, at the end of the steep, narrow lane that starts by climbing over the canal at the eastern end of the village. From the parking area, drag your eyes from the breathtaking view, and follow the level track (the continuation of the lane) to a gate, beyond which a forestry road comes in from the right. Go straight ahead down a short hill and continue for just under 500 metres to reach the stone sign and finger post at Pen Rhiw-calch.

Standing with your back towards the reservoir and the stone sign on your right, the earthy track to the right is the Roman road to Dolygaer, along which you will return, and the rough track to the left is the continuation of that ancient route, along which you will eventually descend, and from where the shorter walk starts. In front is the continuation of the tramroad, along which your journey continues.

Go through the leftmost of the double gates, and follow the obvious track. You will see no stone sleepers here as the tramroad has been buried by forestry workers extracting timber from the plantations ahead, but you can still see the remnants of the original hedge to the right of the track. Go through several gates and continue until you reach a further gate and cattle grid where the forestry track bears left and starts to descend. At this point, go straight on along a much narrower, grassy track with a fence to your left. You are now back on the tramroad with no forestry interference, and will soon see more of the stone sleepers. At the next gate, you enter an extensive clear-felled area where there are the occasional remains of retaining walls to either side of your route (particularly to the right), and good views of the head of the Dyffryn Crawnon and the quarries ahead. At the end of this section, the tramroad curves left on a high embankment over a stream, passes a ruin on the right, and plunges into dense woodland.

I don't know what it is about this part of the tramroad, but if feels totally different to the route through the forestry above Talybont. It has a definite atmosphere – gloomy, spooky. The hawthorns of the original laid hedges have grown huge, old and gnarled; there are ancient trees draped with moss; you can imagine it being used as the set of a gothic horror film. Yet some sections of the tram-

*The tramroad through the clear-felled area. There are the remains of retaining walls and many sleeper stones along this section.*

road here are amazingly well preserved, and it can feel as though you are walking back through time. The further you go, the more impressive an achievement the tramroad becomes – a level (sometimes muddy) ledge cut into the side of an increasingly imposing hillside using only pick axes, wheelbarrows, shovels, and sheer hard graft. The slopes to the left drop more and more steeply; the slopes to the right rear up to be topped with vertical, sometimes overhanging rock outcrops.

The sound of falling water reaches your ears just before the tramroad swings left on an embankment over a cascading stream, a strikingly picturesque spot, and then you reach a short section where the tramroad has subsided, the whole structure slipping bodily down the mountainside. On the far side looms a large cliff, and the tramroad disappears, the original bridge across the Nant Ddu having been swept away by winter floods. Cross the stream bed, on the far side of which a narrow path leads across steep slopes and regains the tramroad at a kissing gate.

You now come to an 'interesting' section, for the tramroad crosses the steep, often precipitous headwall of Cwm Crawnon. This was a dangerous area even when the tramroad was operating – indeed two horses fell to their deaths here in 1855 – but taken steadily, the path is fine. While the drops are never huge, the path has been affected by landslide and rock fall, and you need to take care in places. Watch out for old graffiti – the most obvious being the

*The 'interesting' section of tramroad around the vertical headwall of Cwm Crawnon.*

*The footbridge at the head of Cwm Crawnon, beyond which the character of the walk changes.*

name 'W Lloyd 1894' carved on a flat rock face beside the path not long after you have crossed the Nant Ddu. Keep your eyes open, too, for some amazing trees growing straight out of the cliff, their roots slowly prising apart the bedrock – no wonder there have been rock falls! This awkward section ends at a large gully with limestone outcrops to the right, beyond which you cross a stile. The path now eases but becomes fairly overgrown (beware the nettles if you are wearing shorts) and soon reaches a metal stile and a wooden footbridge.

Beyond the footbridge, there is a dramatic change, not only in the vegetation, but also in the atmosphere. The slopes in front are often littered with rusting, burnt-out cars dumped here by some of South Wales's less enlightened youths, for their dubious amusement. Even after the regular clean-up operations, the evidence is all around – bits of car lie everywhere. It is as if you are standing at a cultural divide. To the left lies the pastoral splendour of mid-Wales – to the right, the wasteland of the quarries and the industrial heartlands of South Wales.

*The ruined limekiln on the side of the tramroad below Hendre Quarry.*

Continue along a rocky, awkward section of tramroad, passing below a large, steep outcrop of grey limestone. The views open out dramatically along this section. You can see across the Dyffryn Crawnon to the eastern Brecon Beacons, and down the valley towards the Black Mountains and the wild moors of Mynydd Llangynidr. There is also a great view of the route you have been following since leaving Pen Rhiw-calch, which gives the journey some perspective. You soon reach the remains of a limekiln on the right.

The tramroad continues towards Trefil Quarries and the industrial valleys of South Wales, but not so your route. Just after passing the limekiln, where the path widens, climb the bank on the right to reach a wide, rough track, on the nearside of which is a large standing stone inscribed with a panorama, naming what you can see. On the far side of the track, large boulders form a picnic table – an invitation to stop and have some refreshment while admiring the views.

Having gazed (and eaten) your fill, walk along the track towards the Hendre Quarry – Cwar yr Hendre (to the left as you are facing the panorama stone), soon merging with a tarmac road which leads between high cliffs

Drowned cars in Hendre Quarry. The square structure on the horizon is a good landmark if you choose to explore the area.

into a ravaged landscape. Follow this road for about 1,500 metres, passing various old quarry structures, to where another tarmac road descends gently from some brick-built buildings, high up on the left. Where this road merges with yours (or would do, were it not for a ditch), note the muddy, rutted track to the right – the route of your onward journey.

The whole of this area is much used by film companies as a location – it featured, for example, in the film of *The Hitch Hiker's Guide to the Galaxy*, and has been extensively used as a set for the *Dr Who* series. The most interesting and enigmatic area is above the ruined buildings, near to the obvious strange tower (a derelict hopper) on the skyline. This can be accessed by walking up the road to the brick buildings, and then climbing the slopes behind them, or by continuing along the main quarry road and bearing left. There are some weird contrasts here. The bare rock of the quarry, strewn with the rubbish of countless fly-tippers, fills the foreground, while the splendour of the distant Brecon Beacons forms a panoramic backdrop beyond the nearby wild and boggy moor. There are depressing patches of total dereliction punctuated by sudden jewels where nature is fast reclaiming her own – it is a very strange place with an equally strange feel, with unexpected drops and crystal clear ponds full of lilies, cars, reeds and tyres. You can easily lose thirty minutes exploring, and the time will not be wasted.

Back at the junction, walk along the rutted, muddy track that leads directly away from the quarries across the boggy moor. The original track has been destroyed by off-roaders, whose vehicles have cut into the soft, peaty surface to such an extent that it is sometimes necessary to make wide detours in order to continue without becoming intimately involved with the bog. What I am certain the drivers do not realise is that they are destroying a very ancient track – one that dates from the fifth or sixth century AD, possibly earlier. The evidence for this lies in the presence of an inscribed stone – an Ogham Stone – which stands by the side of the track some 2 kilometres to the south-west. Ogham Script is a type of runic writing of Irish or Celtic origin, which is believed by many scholars to have been used as a secret language by bards and druids.

Follow the ruts and scars across the moor, the ground soon becoming easier, eventually dropping into a shallow valley where the track curves to the right around the head of Gwaun Nant Ddu, believed to be the

*View east from Pant y Creigiau. The conical summit of Sugar Loaf is just visible on the horizon, just left of centre. The Brinore Tramroad climbs through the forestry beyond the distant Talybont Reservoir.*

site of an ancient lake. The route of the ancient track soon becomes far more obvious, and archaeological excavations have shown it to have had a well-dressed surface between substantial edge stones. It was undoubtedly a route of some importance in the distant past. Continue for just under a kilometre to a junction with another track – a Roman road – at Pen Bwlch Glasgwm.

The Pant y Creigiau Loop adds 7 kilometres plus 100 metres of ascent. Allow 90 minutes. Pant y Creigiau is a fabulous viewpoint at the western end of a ridge of high land to your north. To include this in your walk, leave the ancient track where it curves to the right around the head of Gwaun Nant Ddu, and head straight on (north-west) across the rough moor, eventually reaching another track – the Roman road from Dolygaer. Cross this, then immediately trend left and climb towards the skyline on convenient sheep tracks. Continue in the same direction across

*The view north from the Roman road just beyond Pen Bwlch Glasgwm.*

another shallow valley filled with sedge, then trend left again on more sheep tracks towards the obvious lump of Pant y Creigiau, soon dropping to a shallow saddle and merging with a better path which climbs a short but steeper section from where the trig point comes into view. The views from the trig point are expansive in every direction – you can even see Pen Rhiw-calch and the line of the Brinore Tramroad above the Talybont Reservoir. The only fly in the ointment is the amount of damage that has been done to the surface of the moor by trials bikes.

Leave the trig point along the outward path and return to the saddle, from where an obvious path leads along the centre of the ridge towards Bryniau Gleision, with good views across to the Hendre Quarries. Be careful not to fall into the deep ruts caused by the trials bikes, and look out for the wild ponies! The top of Bryniau Gleision is peppered with grassy hollows and rocky mounds – the remains of very old surface quarries. These are totally different to the Hendre Quarries, having been started in a different age, and having been largely reclaimed by nature.

The path skirts the summit to the right and soon descends to join the obvious rutted route of the Roman road from Dolygaer. Join this and bear left to reach the junction with the ancient track at Pen Bwlch Glasgwm.

As you scramble down the suddenly rocky track at Pen Bwlch Glasgwm, look down to your right to see the Brinore Tramroad as it crosses the clear-felled area just before the head of Cwm Crawnon. At the next gate, you cross from the Dyffryn Crawnon into Glyn Collwn, and the views change accordingly. The track you are now following is a once-important Roman road, one of the few really ancient routes across the Brecon Beacons, and built (more or less) on top of the original ancient track. It steadily descends the ridge separating the two valleys, with wide views across to the eastern slopes of the Brecon Beacons.

At the next gate, the track becomes more level, and you can once again see the Brinore Tramroad to the right, on the opposite side of the

*The Talybont Reservoir dam from the lane below Tor y Foel.*

ridge. The surface of the track becomes increasingly red as it crosses a particularly colourful layer of Old Red Sandstone (this section can get very wet after heavy rain), and after a few bright scarlet puddles, you arrive back at the stone sign at Pen Rhiw-calch. Continue straight ahead on a better surfaced track, soon climbing a short hill to reach a junction. Ignoring the obvious track descending to the left, bear right on to a rough lane, go through a gate, and climb gently to reach more level ground as you approach the car parking area used by the shorter route.

From here, the route back to Talybont is obvious – simply follow the now better-surfaced lane, ignoring all turnings, as it meanders down into the Usk Valley with splendid and extensive views. You are still, most probably, following the line of the ancient track and Roman road, but all evidence is now buried beneath the tarmac. On reaching the canal, cross the bridge and turn left on to the towpath. There is a replica tramcart and an information board here, directly opposite the long line of limekilns which were built at the terminus of the Brinore Tramroad. Lime burnt here was sent along the canal to markets at Brecon, Abergavenny, and further afield, but the original loading area, Overton's Wharf, is now largely overgrown. Continuing along the towpath will take you past (or perhaps into) the beer gardens of the White Hart and Star Inns, and thus back to the iron drawbridge and your car.

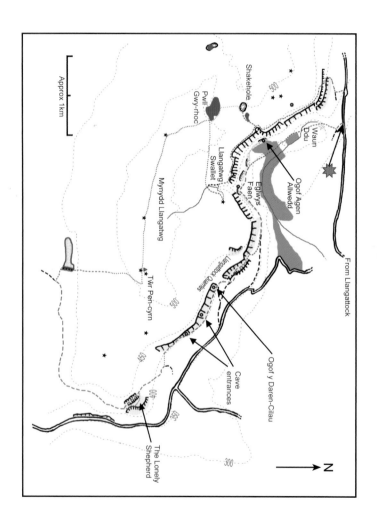

The Lonely Shepherd

The Lonely Shepherd

Cave entrances

Ogof y Daren-Cilau

Llangattock Quarries

Twr Pen-cyrn

Mynydd Llangatwg

Pwll Gwy-rhoc

Shakehole

Llangatwg Swallet

Eglwys Faen

Ogof Agen Allwedd

Waun Ddu

From Llangattock

Approx 1km

N

46

# 3.
# THE HOLLOW MOUNTAIN

A very scenic exploration of the wonders of both human and natural engineering on Mynydd Llangatwg (Llangattock Mountain), high above the Usk Valley, with a battlefield, a haunted lake, Bronze Age burial cairns, ancient (and not so ancient) quarries, tramroads, caves, and breathtaking panoramas.

## BACKGROUND INFORMATION

**Location** Mynydd Llangatwg (Llangattock Mountain), to the south of Crickhowell, on the main A40 between Abergavenny and Brecon (see also Walk 1).

**Start & finish point** Rough lay-by/roadside parking at SO185169, immediately west of the cattle grid on the mountain road from Llangattock village to Blaen Onneu.

**Maps needed** OS Explorer OL13.

**Map distance** 15 kilometres.

**Height gain** 350 metres.

**Terrain** A mixture of paths, varying from excellent to not-so-good, some close to the tops of large vertical drops. The route across the plateau involves ill-defined sheep tracks and cross-country walking on rough, often boggy moorland.

**Duration** Allow 5 hours.

**Hazards** Cliff-edge paths. Boggy terrain and potentially tricky navigation across the plateau. Loose rock and unexpected drops in and around the quarries. Caves.

**Public transport** There is a reasonable bus service to Crickhowell from Abergavenny and Brecon. The nearest railway station is at Abergavenny.

**Amenities/facilities** Crickhowell is a bustling village with a good selection of shops and an inordinate number of excellent hostelries and guesthouses! There are two banks (Lloyds TSB & NatWest) and a post office.

LATE IN THE 1960s, a small group of school friends and I spent a fortnight wandering around the Brecon Beacons National Park on what was supposed to be a 'geological expedition'. It was the first occasion that any of us had been on an unsupervised, extended camping trip in a mountainous region and, to be honest, our enthusiasm for the outdoors got the better of us. The 'expedition' rapidly deteriorated into a veritable orgy of hill walking, climbing and caving, and we ended up spending several days exploring the adrenaline-fuelled delights of the magnificent Llangattock Escarpment – a sinuous line of impressive limestone cliffs and melancholy quarries which stretches for a distance of about 12 kilometres. The more we explored, the more I fell in love with the place, and despite the naivety of adolescence, I had a profound sense that here was an area in which I could happily settle down. Little did I guess that, almost exactly a decade later, chance would lead me to put down my roots less than 5 kilometres from where we pitched our tents!

Mynydd Llangatwg (Llangattock Mountain) is a huge lump of limestone in the south-eastern corner of the Brecon Beacons National Park. Capped with gritstone and peat, honeycombed with some of the longest cave systems in Britain, and with its edges nibbled away by past quarrying, it rises between the industrial valleys of South Wales and the pastoral splendour of mid-Wales forming not only a physical barrier, but also something of a cultural divide. The Llangattock Escarpment runs around the eastern and northern edges of the mountain, and the central section – containing Llangattock Quarries and the Craig y Cilau National Nature Reserve – forms the skyline to the south of Llangattock, towering over the village and rivalling the slopes of the Black Mountains on the opposite side of the Usk Valley. The vertical gash of the Clydach Gorge, a birthplace of the Welsh iron industry, forms the southern boundary, while to the west, the high moors of the summit plateau merge into those of Mynydd Llangynidr (Llangynidr Mountain), the boundary being the B4560 – the highest B road in Wales – which crosses the mountain from north to south.

It is a place of opposites – of flat, boggy moorland and precipitous limestone cliffs; of untrammelled mountain wildness and the hand of man. Two hundred years ago, the area echoed with the ring of hammer on stone, and a complex network of tramroads and inclines connected busy quarries to both the ironworks to the south and the canal to the north. A century before that, rugged packhorses bred from wild Welsh ponies plodded up and down the slopes carrying lime from the quarries

*The view east from above Craig y Castell. The line of a tramroad is obvious below the cliffs.*

to the acid fields of the Usk Valley. Five hundred years and more before the packhorses, local people chipped away at the surface rocks in order to obtain building materials for their dwellings, and in the preceding millennia, opposing Celtic tribes fought bloody battles here and left lasting memorials to their dead. It is a superbly atmospheric place and is, without doubt, one of my favourite areas.

The walk starts from a cattle grid on the surprisingly busy unclassified road which links the villages of Crickhowell and Llangattock to the B4560 mountain road between Llangynidr and Beaufort, and thus to the infamous Heads of the Valleys Road and the industrial south. The traditional heavy industries of the South Wales Valleys have been decimated over the past few decades, and there is much funding available to encourage new business to the area. The pit head baths and steel yards have been transformed into technology parks and industrial estates; the coal merchants and iron foundries replaced by telecommunications, pharmaceuticals, and computer software companies. While local labour is cheap, technical expertise is at a premium, so 'experts' are often recruited from outside the area. These newcomers want to work in the valleys because of the incentives, but many wish to live in mid-Wales because of the scenery and the perceived quality of life. The nearest desirable housing is thus in the Usk Valley (which explains why property is so expensive in and around Crickhowell) and they commute to and from work each day (which explains why the mountain road is so busy).

Having secured your car, walk uphill alongside the road for a couple of hundred metres to reach a large, rough lay-by on the right, near the brow of a hill. Directly opposite, a narrow, sometimes overgrown and ill-defined path leads uphill towards obvious cliffs, soon reaching an old, slightly sunken quarry track. Follow this to the right to reach an area of grassy spoil – the result of past quarrying – then scramble carefully up the messy path that climbs around the right-hand end of the cliffs. Do not follow the obvious cliff-top route, but trend right on an ill-defined, rocky path that climbs past low limestone outcrops to reach a level terrace, then follow the more obvious continuation as it climbs through heather and whin towards the skyline.

The view at the top is as unexpected as it is sudden. A breathtaking amphitheatre of limestone cliffs towers above the lush Cwm Onneu Fach – a small valley totally hidden from the road – while in the distance, the shapely Sugar Loaf sits in splendid isolation above Abergavenny. Waun Ddu, a lozenge-shaped bog, 150 almost vertical metres below your feet, lies slumped at the top of the narrow valley, the headwall of which is formed by a sharp spur which descends steeply to the parking area. The views over the Usk Valley and the Black Mountains beyond are nothing short of spectacular. This is an impressive spot.

Continue along the path that hugs the edge of the escarpment, ignoring all paths veering off to the right, soon dropping into a wide but shallow valley where there are the scant ruins of what was probably a shepherd's shelter. Keep straight ahead on the sometimes awkward edge path as it crosses the valley mouth then climbs the far side, eventually passing numerous blocks that look remarkably like concrete! These are, in fact, boulders of a rock called basal conglomerate, a type of gritstone that lies at the boundary of the Carboniferous Limestone (below) and the Millstone Grit (above). The round white pebbles are water-worn vein quartz, held in a matrix of coarse sandstone.

The path soon levels out, skirts the top of an exceptionally steep, rounded, grassy gully with impressive views down to the valley floor, and then continues straight ahead with the tops of trees growing from the cliff face visible to the left. There are several excellent viewpoints along here, but be aware that there is an awesome vertical drop beyond! The path then curves to the right to avoid a large, precipitous gully that cuts into the escarpment ahead, and enters a small, shallow valley.

It is worth making a slight detour here. Instead of following the main path back to the edge, turn right along the valley floor on a less well-defined path which leads almost immediately to an intermittent pool, its peat bed sometimes dry and dusty, sometimes wet and boggy. Beyond, to the left of the obvious sloping boulder field, lies an immense crater. This is an exceptionally large example of a shakehole, formed when the surface rocks collapsed into a cavern. In wet weather, two sizeable streams pour into this hole, their waters immediately disappearing through the rocks to reappear in the vast Agen Allwedd cave system below, the base of the collapsed rocks forming an area of the cave known as the First Boulder

*Sugar Loaf from the edge of the huge shakehole. The peaty bed of the intermittent pool is obvious just right of centre.*

*On the edge – walking the cliff-top path in atmospheric conditions.*

Choke. You will learn more about this and other cave systems, later in the walk.

If you wish, you can shorten the walk at this point, for by heading due south you will reach Pwll Gwy-rhoc after only 400 metres, thus reducing the length of the walk by about 2 kilometres. However, the ground is very boggy and you will miss one of the best viewpoints of the entire walk!

Retrace your steps past the intermittent pool and turn right on to the main path, soon regaining the escarpment edge with stunning views across the Usk Valley to the Black Mountains and beyond. Just beyond the next small valley, the path levels out along the top of some crumbling cliffs, and then forces its way through clumps of sedge before beginning a gradual descent towards the obvious deep, narrow valley that slashes its way into the hillside in front. Do not descend, but turn left on to a level area of whin and heather – the promontory – where you will find some of the best views of the day.

Now comes a tricky bit. Your objective is the obvious stone cairn on the opposite side of the narrow valley that cuts into the plateau to the

*ABOVE* View west from the promontory.

*RIGHT* View east from the promontory.

53

*Llangatwg Swallett – a thorn in the sides of generations of cavers. The stream disappears through boulders (to the left of the person wearing a red hat), and is not seen again until it reappears on the far side of the mountain.*

east. The best way to reach this is to follow a reasonable path that runs along the top of the western side of the valley until you reach a large, bouldery shakehole. Follow an indistinct (some may say invisible) path which curves around the left side of this, eventually picking up a not-much-better path which leads across the slopes beyond and drops steeply down a short spur to reach a wide depression in the valley floor – the enigmatic Llangatwg Swallet. In all but the driest weather, a musical mountain stream comes rushing down to this point, only to disappear through the boulders. Generations of cavers have tried to find their way underground here, for the water disappears into a hitherto unexplored part of the massive cave system which exists below your feet, and is not seen again until it reappears in the bottom of the Clydach Gorge, on the opposite side of the mountain! If you put your ear to the ground, you can hear the water falling; and there must be air connections because bats fly in and out between the rocks at dawn and dusk. But the way into the caves through the tangle of boulders is elusive.

*Pwll Gwy-rhoc at dusk – an eerie, brooding place, even in the light of day.*

To reach the cairn, walk up the valley for a few metres, then follow the faint path that heads back and up the left side of the valley to reach a level terrace. The cairn is obvious on the skyline, but the way to reach it is neither obvious nor straightforward, involving a modicum of scrambling over loose boulders. I leave the final choice of route to you! The cairn itself is all that remains of an ancient burial chamber, one of many on this part of mountain, and one that is almost certainly associated with a ancient battle – more of which anon.

Your next objective – Pwll Gwy-rhoc – is not so obvious, for it lies hidden in the middle of the plateau and is impossible to see until you are quite close. Follow the faint path that leads from the cairn along the left side of the valley, cross the stream at the far end, then climb on to the plateau and walk due west for 800 metres. Mind the bog – especially after wet weather.

Pwll Gwy-rhoc is a eerie place – it gives me the creeps. I once camped alone by its shores and awoke in the depths of the night in a cold sweat. The malevolence was almost tangible – nothing would have persuaded me to leave the tent, or even to have looked out of the entrance! Even on bright, sunny days it has a brooding atmosphere, and my shoulder blades always clench when I walk away. Known locally as the Witches' Pool, the water is sometimes blood red, and is never still. Legend has it that back in the Dark Ages, a bloody battle was fought on the mountain between two of the five great tribes of Wales, and the lake is supposed to be located in the same place as the centre of the battle. According to the legend, the ground became so trampled and poisoned with blood and gore that the vegetation never recovered, and the area slowly sank into the bog and became a lake. If you stand on the shore and look at the near horizon through 360°, every high point has (or had) a burial cairn on it. The stuff of legends, perhaps, but it is now accepted in scholarly circles that a great battle really was fought here in AD 728, between Ethelbald the Mercian and the men of Morgannwg led by Rhoderic Molwynog. The Mercians were heavily defeated in what ancient manuscripts describe as a blood bath. There is seldom smoke without fire!

From the lake, head south-east on to the drier, higher ground of the ridge, soon getting fine views towards the South Wales Valleys. Follow the ridge eastwards past the remains of several cairns, eventually reaching the summit of the mountain at Twr Pen-cyrn, where there is a trig point

*The wide expanse of Mynydd Llangatwg from Twr Pen-cyrn. The twin summits of the Brecon Beacons are just visible on the horizon.*

and the remains of two large burial cairns, one of which is known to have contained the remains of a large, Celtic warrior. The views here are superb in every direction, and the cairns offer plenty of shelter if it is windy.

Having explored the ancient Iron Age of two millennia ago, the next part of the walk involves the more modern Iron Age of two centuries ago. Leave the summit by scrambling carefully down the rocky slopes to the east, then turn right on to a faint path that hugs the base of the steep slopes and leads in a more-or-less southerly direction. It has to be admitted that this path is not the best, so check your compass every now and then and keep heading just west of south, until you see a small, drained reservoir ahead (shown as being full of water on OS maps). Gain the dam (often awkwardly muddy), cross it, turn left on the far side, and make for the obvious track that crosses the hillside in front via a narrow corridor through the fenced-off area.

You are now following the route of an old tramroad, built to carry limestone from the Darren Disgwylfa quarries to important ironworks at Nantyglo. The documentation about this tramroad is very sparse. Although it is not know when it was constructed, it is certain that it was in existence by 1818, which makes it the oldest tramroad on the mountain. A plateway with a gauge of 2 feet 4 inches, most of the southern section is now long gone, buried under Brynmawr and the Heads

*Beyond the boggy sections, the Darren Disgwylfa tramroad is in a remarkably good state of repair.*

*The Darren Disgwylfa tramroad – a ribbon of green across the hillside.*

of the Valleys road. The northern section, however, is in a remarkably good state of repair, as you will discover once you have negotiated four short gaps where the original track has sunk into the bog. These start just after the corridor between the fences (the first being the worst), and are best passed to the left. Look for the continuation of the tramroad before you detour so you can regain it more easily on the far side of each gap.

Once the tramroad leaves the bog and traverses drier, more rocky hillside, it offers easy walking with stupendous views to the east. You gaze across Abergavenny and Gilwern, the Sugar Loaf and the Blorenge, Gilwern Hill and the Skirrid, the Clydach Gorge and the Usk Valley. Your route takes you through shallow cuttings and over low embankments, and there are regular foundation stones on which the spreader bars (the tramroad equivalent to sleepers) were placed. Later, where the ground becomes steeper, the tramroad becomes a shelf across the slope, and then, shortly after passing a lonely house down on the right, you reach a three-way junction. Take great care here, for the rightmost track leads straight to the top of a sheer, quarried cliff that appears without warning across your path. The cliff obviously post-dates the tramroad, the lower quarry not being opened until the late 1800s or early 1900s, by which

*Darren Disgwylfa Quarry and the Lonely Shepherd.*

time the top tramroad was no longer in use. However, by approaching this sudden and dramatic end with care, and then turning left along the cliff edge, you can reach the original quarries where there is a local landmark – the Lonely Shepherd – an unquarried pinnacle of limestone which was left in place so that the land owner could gauge how much material had been removed.

The landscape here, and that to the south and south-west, has been hugely shaped by the hand of man. Wherever you look, vast quantities of stone have been removed from the hillsides to feed the ravenous appetites of the ironworks. Yet although man has shaped the landscape, he has not tamed it! Nature is fast reclaiming her own, and the area has a paradoxically wild feel.

Back at the junction, you can follow either the leftmost or the central track as they eventually lead to the same place. The leftmost track takes you into an overgrown cutting – a fine example of a trench quarry – with a breach in the wall ahead. It was through here that the original tramroad was extended to reach the Llangattock Quarries in the distance. The central track leads up and around the northern side of the trench, meeting the extension beyond the breach. This whole area was extensively quarried during the nineteenth century, and there are many possible onward paths. Just keep heading towards the obvious cliffs in the distance – the first of the Llangattock Quarries – eventually meeting a more modern, stony track that descends to a gap in a fenced corridor – the route of a gas pipeline. Follow the track into the gap, but not around the bend, instead exiting straight ahead to reach a narrow and often overgrown path (no better than a sheep track), which climbs gently towards the base of the cliffs in front.

Below you at this point, a narrow mountain road traverses the hillside. This has been laid on the course of another tramroad, built in 1831 to link Llangattock Quarries to the Nantyglo Ironworks. You will follow the spectacular far end of this later. The all-too-obvious eyesore near the road junction below is a gas repressurising station. Not only is this a hideous intrusion in such a scenic place, but the laying of the pipeline has destroyed all the industrial archaeology across a wide corridor, such that the original route of the upper tramroad is long gone. Once you reach the base of the cliffs, you are back on the line of a tramroad again, although it is impossible to tell whether this is the same tramroad as you were following earlier. Although it is known that the Daren Disgwylfa tramroad was extended towards Llangattock Quarries, little is known about its exact route, and the levels here seem all wrong. The situation is further confused by the fact that the tramroad you are now following soon ends, forcing you to climb an obvious sheep track across some spoil in order to reach another tramroad at a slightly higher level. A look at the 1891 Ordnance Survey map of the area does little to help as it shows a plethora of tramroads.

The upper tramroad was obviously a major route linking all the quarries along this section of the escarpment. Over the next kilometre and a half, you pass numerous quarried bays, several of which have mounds of spoil or unquarried rock left to provide shelter from the weather. The quarrying here was totally unlike the surgical precision of modern quarries – there were no high explosives and mechanical aids, only black powder and sheer hard graft. The way in which the stone was removed was fairly basic. The quarrymen would start by drilling shot-holes, the remains of which can still be seen in places along the base of the cliffs. The drill was a long iron bar with a hardened end, and this was held in place by one man while another hit it repeatedly with a sledge hammer, the drill being turned through about 90° after each blow. When the required depth was reached, a charge of black powder was inserted and lit, and the resulting explosion – a slow and gentle blast by today's standards – shattered the rock sufficiently for the men to start removing it with crow bars. These explosions often only shattered the rock at the base of the cliffs, resulting in the formation of large overhangs which were temporarily held in place with wooden props. When the overhangs became too big, the quarrymen set fire to the props, the resulting heat cracking the rock causing it to shatter and, hopefully, fall to the floor. Sometimes the rock would collapse early, and deaths and injuries from falling rock were commonplace. At other times, the rock would shatter but not fall, and quarrymen were then forced to hang chains down the quarry-face and climb down, prising away the loose rock with crow bars while hanging from the chain. Life was cheap.

Many of the rock faces hereabouts contain cave entrances, and one in particular is worth visiting. Towards the end of this section, after the tramroad has levelled and widened, are the remains of an old, brick-built limekiln below and to the right, just before a junction where a stony track curves in from the right. At this point, leave the main tramroad and walk back and to the left along a cutting through the spoil, passing a large, rectangular block of limestone before emerging at the quarry floor. Trend slightly right along a faint path, heading straight towards the base of the large, tufa-encrusted cliff. Here you will find a small depression with an even smaller hole leading beneath the cliff and on, into the depths of the mountain. This is the entrance to Ogof y Daren-Cilau (known to cavers simply as Darren), and it is possible to enter here and come out on the other side of the mountain. If you crouch down and shine a torch along the passage you will get some idea of what extreme caving is like, for what you are seeing is the largest part of the cave for over 600 metres. The passage then gets bigger – much bigger – and leads into an astonishing system containing over 30 kilometres of passage, including the breath-taking Time Machine, a huge passage well over 30 metres wide and 45 metres high. Here is a landscape within a landscape, an environment totally alien to most, but cherished by the cavers who delight in exploring the 'Great Indoors'! Formed entirely by rainwater slowly dissolving the rock, the caves under this mountain are among the most extensive in Britain.

Back on the main path, ignore the stony track curving to the right past the limekiln, instead bearing slightly left along a gently descending straight section of grassy tramroad, soon merging with another stony

*Approaching Pinnacle Bay. The tramroad enters the bay via
a steep-sided cutting through the conical spoil heaps.*

track coming in from the right near a large, rectangular stone tank, once
a water reservoir for the cottages on the hillside below. Continue slightly
left, then curve hard left into a cutting and enter a large quarried bay
where you should turn right and follow the track between the cliffs and
the spoil. This is Pinnacle Bay, part of the large Pant-y-Rhiw Quarry,
an area which, in the mid-1980s, was popular with climbing groups
and was often full of fun and laughter. I don't know how many children
(and adults) were introduced to rock climbing here, but it must run into
thousands. During most school holidays, local campsites were full of
scouts and other organised groups who visited because of the wealth of
activities available in the immediate area, and money poured into the
local economy as they bought provisions and sought entertainment and
adventure. The National Park Authority even had a car park built on the
hillside to accommodate the numerous cars and minibuses. But it was

not to last. While most groups were well-led and well-behaved, some were not, and a small cabal of local graziers used the misbehaviour as an excuse to try and get climbing and other outdoor pursuits banned ... and so began a long-running and bitter access dispute, the ramifications of which are still around today. Huge amounts of ill-will and mistrust were generated, and the visiting groups – quite understandably – stopped coming. Nor have they returned, even though the area is now designated as Access Land, because no one wants to bring a group to an area where they might still receive abuse and threats from one or two local people – the self-styled 'kings of the mountain', ring-leaders of the original dispute. I estimate that over the past fifteen or so years, the whole sorry affair has lost the local economy well in excess of a million pounds!

At the end of the bay, the track swings right into another cutting. Ignore this and, instead, carry straight on alongside the base of the cliff, which soon gets higher with an impressive line of overhangs just below half height, giving some of the finest rock climbing in the National Park. Continue along a low ridge of spoil, then trend to the right to reach a level track, which you follow to the left to reach a large bay littered with cubic boulders – the remains of a massive rockfall that occurred in 1948. I was once told that many quarrymen were killed by this rockfall – probably an apocryphal tale, as the quarries had long since closed. Take care around here, as the rock is still unstable and small falls are common.

Just beyond the cubes of layered limestone, the ground falls away, and a narrow, gravel path curves from left to right down the steep slope. Follow this and turn left at the bottom on to a faint path across more grassy spoil and then along the right side of a cutting, soon descending to a wide, level track traversing the steep mountainside. This is the far end of the Nantyglo to Llangattock Quarries tramroad, seen earlier as the mountain road. Bear left, walk round the corner, and enter the Craig y Cilau National Nature Reserve. The views are stunning.

Craig y Cilau is one of the more outstanding botanical sites in Wales, with many rare plants and birds as well as impressive geological and geomorphological features. Although it is perhaps best known for its rare endemic *Sorbus* species (the lesser whitebeam, *Sorbus minima*, is unique to this area), the reserve is equally important for its hawkweeds, of which there are at least fifteen. *Hieracium cillense* (Craig y Cilau hawkweed),

*The Craig y Cilau National Nature Reserve, with the tramroad obvious along the base of the cliffs. The numerous entrances to the Eglwys Faen cave system lie in the rock buttress left of centre, where the tramroad curves to the right. The entrance to Agen Allwedd is at the far end of the tramroad.*

and *Hieracium asteridiophyllum* (Llangattock hawkweed), in particular, are very rare, believed to be confined to the area around the Reserve.

The wide, grassy tramroad offers easy access into what would otherwise be a wild and difficult area. Just before it swings to the right and clips a rock buttress, a quarried bay contains the foundations of an old weigh-house, and it is here that you will begin to see the several entrances to the Eglwys Faen cave system, one directly in front of you, two high up at the back of the bay, another hidden at the base of the small waterfall which, in all but the driest weather, spills over the lip of the small spur to the left. There are two more entrances in the face of the buttress (be warned: the larger, upper one has an unexpected drop just inside), another around the far side, and if you scramble up the steep, loose zigzag path beyond the buttress, you will come to the main entrance, which leads directly into the large main chamber. Eglwys Faen, translated, means Stone Church, and this chamber was used (reputedly by the Quakers) both as a place of refuge and as a church during times of religious persecution. The

Chartists are also thought to have had a small forge in the further reaches of the main chamber where they made weapons prior to their march on Newport in 1839 (although this may be a confusion with another site – Chartist Cave – which lies on Mynydd Llangynidr to the west).

There are currently almost 2 kilometres of explored passage in this system, but cavers know that there must be much more awaiting discovery – indeed, many believe that this cave contains the missing link that will help join together all the other cave systems under the mountain. The water from Llangattock Swallet, for example, is believed to enter the cave beyond the boulder choke that marks the present end of the main passage – the water can be heard, but no way on has yet been found, despite many hours of effort. While there is little to prevent you exploring a short way, be aware that the rocks are very slippery, and please do not go beyond the daylight unless you really are properly equipped. Having a torch does not mean you are properly equipped.

A short distance beyond Eglwys Faen, the tramroad has been washed away by winter storms, but it is a simple matter to cross the gap and rejoin

*The tramroad offers delightfully easy walking into the precipitous heart of the Craig y Cilau National Nature Reserve.*

*The gated entrance to the vast Ogof Agen Allwedd. Known as Aggy to cavers, the whole cave system has been designated as an SSSI. The gate shown in this picture (taken in 1988) has now been replaced by a more modern structure.*

it on the far side, continuing into the heart of the reserve with its increasingly impressive limestone cliffs. About 250 metres beyond the break, at a point where the tramroad swings to the left at the end of another quarried bay, a rough, narrow, waymarked path leads steeply down to the right.

Although the main route lies along this path, by continuing for a further 400 metres to the end of tramroad, you will reach a low cliff in which there is a gated cave entrance. This is Ogof Agen Allwedd, a huge cave system with over 35 kilometres of explored passage. The whole system has been designated an SSSI, and parts of the cave are home to one of the largest roosts of lesser horseshoe bats in Britain. Access is freely available to bona fide cavers – the gate is there to prevent access by the unwary or ill-equipped. Work is ongoing to try and connect Ogof Agen Allwedd with Ogof y Daren Cilau, with Eglwys Faen, and with another huge cave, Ogof Craig-a-ffynnon, the entrance to which is above the Clydach Gorge on the southern side of the mountain. While it is possible to regain the main route by descending the slopes opposite the entrance, the ground is steep, rough and awkward, and it is probably quicker (and certainly easier) to retrace your steps to the waymarked path.

Follow the waymarked path as it meanders down the hillside, bearing left at the next waymarked junction. Continue through ancient woodland, the path rough and awkward in places, eventually emerging into more open terrain where the path eases and descends to an old stone wall and trees. Bear left alongside the wall to reach the dome-shaped Waun Ddu, cross the stream, and walk over the dome towards an obvious path leading up the headwall on the far side.

Waun Ddu is an excellent example of a raised bog, formed when a build up of peat causes the living surface of the bog to rise above the surrounding land. Although heavily grazed, the Countryside Council for Wales have fenced three small areas in order to investigate what the vegetation would be like if there were no sheep. The differences are obvious and remarkable – nothing has been planted (the trees, for example, are self-seeded); the areas have simply been kept ungrazed for several years.

The far end of the bog is often wet and awkward to cross – the easiest route is opposite the lowest end of the leftmost of the two paths that climb the headwall. The paths eventually merge and climb steeply past another Nature Reserve information board – pause here to catch your breath and admire the view behind, then continue alongside the wall and fence to reach a good track where the views open out again to the north. Turn left and follow the track for less than 100 metres to reach the cattle grid from where you started.

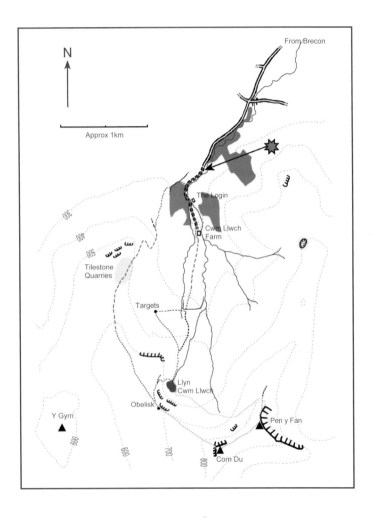

# 4.
# IN THE FOOTSTEPS OF TOMMY JONES

A stunningly scenic walk centred on an unspoilt valley, involving the mystery of a lost five-year-old, a haunted lake and a disused army rifle range, all in the heart of the Brecon Beacons. An optional extension allows you to visit the highest mountain in southern Britain.

## BACKGROUND INFORMATION

**Location** In the heart of the central Brecon Beacons, immediately north of the two highest peaks – Pen y Fan and Corn Du.

**Start & finish point** Rough parking area at SO006245, near Llwynbedw.

**Maps needed** OS Explorer OL12; Harvey Superwalker – Brecon Beacons East.

**Map distance** 9 kilometres.

**Height gain** 400 metres.

The optional extension taking in the summits of Corn Du and Pen y Fan adds 4 kilometres of map distance and a further 250 metres of ascent.

**Terrain** Excellent paths for the most part, although the main path down the centre of Cwm Llwch can be muddy in parts after very wet weather. The direct descent from the summit of Pen y Fan involves some very steep ground.

**Duration** Allow 3 hours for the main walk or 5 hours for the extended walk.

**Hazards** Steep, awkward ground on the direct descent from Pen y Fan – a serious undertaking in winter conditions. Standard mountain safety precautions apply.

**Public transport** Brecon is served by several bus services. The nearest railway stations are at Merthyr Tydfil and Abergavenny.

**Amenities/facilities** Brecon is a busy tourist and farming centre with all the amenities you would expect of a market town, including an excellent Tourist Information Centre, leisure centre, and theatre.

ON A WINDSWEPT RIDGE, high on the slopes of the mightiest peaks of the Brecon Beacons and overlooking the legend-swathed waters of Llyn Cwm Llwch, stands a lonely granite obelisk. Erected over a century ago, it marks the spot where the remains of five-year-old Tommy

Jones were found after he had been missing for twenty-nine days. His sudden disappearance is still shrouded in uncertainty, and the curious events which led to his eventual discovery simply add to the air of mystery. The only thing certain about the whole affair is that no one will ever know exactly what happened.

The story of little Tommy Jones has fascinated me for years. The first serious research I did was in 1984, when I was commissioned to write a piece about the story for a magazine. At the time, my son was five years old, the same age as Tommy, and this gave an added poignancy to the research. Since then I have wandered through Cwm Llwch on countless occasions, and each time I visit, I invariably find myself thinking about Tommy. Of course, we will never know what really happened to him, and any investigation is hampered by the fact that the paths and tracks have all changed considerably in the intervening hundred years.

Before you follow the walk, you should know something of the story. This begins early on 4 August 1900 – a sultry Bank Holiday Saturday – at Maerdy, a mining village at the northern end of the Rhondda Fach valley. William Jones, a miner from the Maerdy Colliery, decided to take his five-year-old son, Tommy, to visit his grandparents, who farmed near Brecon. This would have been quite an adventure for Tommy, who had never before travelled far from his home among the terraces and coal tips of the mining valleys. Leaving early in the morning, they travelled to Merthyr Tydfil (at that time, the largest town in Wales) where they boarded a train. This took them through lonely valleys and untamed mountains, eventually arriving in Brecon at about six o'clock that evening. Hot and tired after their journey, they then started the 6-kilometre walk to Cwm Llwch Farm where Tommy's grandparents lived, no doubt looking forward to a warm welcome.

Some two hours later, just before eight o'clock, they reached the Login where a company of soldiers were camped while training at the nearby rifle range. In need of refreshment, William Jones stopped for a drink at the canteen, and he bought Tommy a pennyworth of biscuits as a special treat. As luck, or fate, would have it, Tommy's grandfather strolled by as they were resting, accompanied by thirteen-year-old Willie John, Tommy's cousin. As William had not yet finished his drink, the two men stayed at the camp and sent Willie John to the farmhouse, less than 500 metres

*The flat summit of Corn Du from the parking area. Tommy Jones's body was eventually found at the extreme right end of the skyline ridge.*

away, to warn of the imminent arrival of guests. Tommy decided to accompany him, so they ran off together along the well-defined track.

Although they had to cross two rough plank bridges not far from the Login, the journey was not particularly difficult, even for a tired five-year-old, but it must have been quite frightening for a young boy whose home was in the back-to-back housing of an industrial valley. Twilight was starting to fall, the trees and streams would have seemed eerie, and any farm animals seen along the way must have appeared like monsters from a fairy tale. No one will ever know exactly what his thoughts were, but the two boys had travelled less than half the distance to the farmhouse when Tommy started to cry and wanted to go back to his father.

And so they parted. Willie John ran to the farm leaving Tommy to travel back to the Login, less than 250 metres away, by himself. Having delivered his message, Willie John returned to the Login, arriving less than fifteen minutes after he had first left, and less than ten minutes since he and Tommy had parted. He had expected to find Tommy either *en route* or with his father ... but there was no sign of him. Immediately they learned what had happened, William and Tommy's grandfather set off along the track to search. Twenty minutes later, having returned to the Login, they were joined in their search by the soldiers, but even though it was impossible that Tommy could have travelled far, not a trace was found.

The search was called off at midnight, but it started again in a far more orderly fashion at 3.00 a.m. on the Sunday, the search parties now including the police, soldiers and members of the public. Believing it to be unlikely that Tommy had gone past the farm, and more probable that he had missed the turning into the Login and continued down the valley, the search was concentrated in that area. It continued until dark, but there was still no sign, so it resumed early the next day.

During the ensuing weeks, a huge number of people including troops, police, farmers, local residents and other volunteers, systematically combed the area. Undergrowth was beaten down in the surrounding woodland, bracken was cut, streams were searched, and local people were questioned. Someone even suggested dragging Llyn Cwm Llwch, but no one thought it possible that a five-year-old, alone and afraid, could have travelled that far up the mountain. It was thought far more likely that he had fallen off one of the bridges, or wandered past the Login and on down the valley. The search, therefore, was concentrated in what was then difficult countryside between the Login and Brecon. Eventually, the idea of kidnap was aired, and with this suggestion came the involvement of the national press. Initially, the blame was laid at the feet of the numerous gypsies who, at that time, were camped throughout South East Wales. All their camps were brusquely searched by the police, but to no avail.

The *Daily Mail* offered £20 (a princely sum in those days) to anyone who could solve the puzzle, this reward being announced in the paper, on posters, and by the Brecon Town Crier. Suggestions and reports of sightings came flooding in from far and wide, and the public response became so great that the paper appointed a Special Commissioner who won much respect in the area. After careful investigation, he decided that kidnapping by gypsies was unlikely but that the boy may well have been snatched by a childless couple or spinster. Therein lay the only hope that Tommy might still be alive.

During all this time, William Jones remained at Cwm Llwch farmhouse, going out with the search parties each day. Eventually his friends persuaded him he could do no further good by staying in the area, and he returned to his home in Maerdy. He did, however, return on numerous occasions, and was among one of the groups that climbed to the top of the Brecon Beacons as the despondent searchers covered increasingly wider areas. After three weeks of intensive searching there was not even the slightest clue as to how little Tommy had so completely disappeared.

Several days passed.

The eventual discovery of Tommy's body is as mysterious as his disappearance. Just under four weeks after the initial incident, a Mrs Hamer, the wife of a gardener from Castle Madoc (a large house about 10 kilometres north of Brecon), had a vivid, recurring dream. Although she had never visited the Brecon Beacons, she dreamt she saw the ridge running from Corn Du (the second highest peak of the Beacons) towards Pen Milan (the wild spur overlooking the Login and the farm). At a point directly above Llyn Cwm Llwch she saw the body of a young boy.

On Sunday 2 September, after two or three worried days and sleepless nights, she finally persuaded her husband (who had visited the Beacons on several previous occasions, and recognised the scene) to take her and some relatives to the area. They walked past Cwm Llwch Farm, up to Llyn Cwm Llwch, and then scrambled steeply up on to the ridge, aiming for a spot chosen by Mrs Hamer. There, to their horror, they found the remains of a small body. It was carried down and identified that day. Mr Hamer had not thought that their trip would yield any information about Tommy, but subsequent reports of the discovery gave him most of the credit. No mention was made of his wife's dream, nor of the fact that she persuaded him to go on the trip in the first place.

At the inquest, which was held on the following Tuesday, there was a unanimous verdict of 'death by exhaustion and exposure', but no one could explain how five-year-old Tommy, having already had a long and tiring day, had reached a point 685 metres above sea level, almost 400 metres above the Login, and over 3 kilometres distant (as the crow flies) across extremely difficult terrain, and in the dark.

The inquest jurors were so moved by the story that they all gave their fees to start a memorial fund. Mr Hamer donated part of his reward money, and many other people, both local and from afar, sent in contributions.

The money was used to pay for a granite memorial stone. Finished in July, 1901, this was then hauled into position on a horse-drawn, wooden sled. The inscription on the stone, now showing signs of a century's worth of exposure to mountain weather, reads:

> This obelisk marks the spot where the body of Tommy Jones, aged 5, was found. He lost his way between Cwm Llwch Farm and the Login, on the night of August 4th, 1900. After an anxious search of 29 days his remains were discovered September 2nd. Erected by voluntary subscriptions. W Powell Price, Mayor of Brecon 1901.

Since then, various answers to the mystery have been postulated – a task made more difficult because, in order to be anywhere near realistic, it is necessary to put yourself into the mind of a frightened five-year-old. I believe the most likely explanation is that Tommy, returning to the Login after having left Willie John, got confused between left and right – after all, I doubt that a five-year-old would recognise that having turned left on the outward journey, he would have to turn right on the return journey. Having crossed the first bridge, he then missed the turning over the second footbridge, following instead what must have been a fairly obvious path used by the soldiers on their way to the rifle range. Sooner or later he realised that he was on the wrong path, but his feelings of confusion and panic grew as he heard muffled shouts behind him as the initial search got underway. Emerging from the narrow band of woods, he would have seen, almost directly in front of him, an obvious track zigzagging up the hillside on its way to the tilestone quarries. Having been told that his grandparents 'lived on a mountain', he may well have thought that by continuing to climb he would eventually reach the farm. In any event, alone and afraid, he carried on until he collapsed from exhaustion.

We will, of course, never know for certain which route Tommy took, and even if we did, we could not follow it today for the layout of the land has changed significantly. The original track from the present day car park to the Login is all but lost (the current track hardly existed in the early 1900s), the two rough plank footbridges have long gone, and the path to the rifle range has disappeared. The following route is thus the closest walkable approximation to what I consider to be the most likely route taken by Tommy on that fateful night.

The best approach to the parking area (and probably the route walked by Tommy and his father) is along Ffrwdgrech Road, which leaves the main road opposite The Drovers pub at the western end of Brecon. Although this starts as a residential street, you soon pass under the by-pass and leave the housing behind. At the first junction take the middle road, then continue straight on for some distance until you reach an offset cross-roads. Continue straight on to the end of the lane, where a gate gives access to the rough parking area. Tommy and his father walked to this point from Brecon railway station, the site of which is now occupied by the main town car park, arriving at about 7.45 p.m.

The original track to the Login veered off to the left at the start of the parking area, crossed the stream (there is still a bridge), then headed more or less straight to the Login alongside the left bank of the stream. Although long gone, traces of a walled lane are still visible in places.

*Frosty morning in Cwm Llwch. Tommy must have made his way across this area before meeting the quarry track that zigzags up the bulk of Pen Milan, to the left. The soldiers' paths have long since disappeared.*

Although it will be necessary to retrace some of your steps, it is useful to get to the Login in order to set the scene, so walk along the main track with the stream to your left until you reach another stream coming in from the right, where there is a ford and modern wooden footbridge – a replacement of the second plank bridge that Tommy crossed. To the left at this point is a black corrugated iron barn – this is the site of the Login, and the army encampment was in the adjacent field. Tommy and his father approached this from the left (notice the remains of the walled lane).

Originally, another footbridge crossed the main stream immediately downstream of the confluence. Although this is long gone, there is still evidence of the buttresses on either bank. Tommy and Willie John crossed the (now missing) plank bridge, immediately turned left, crossed another plank bridge (where the modern bridge now stands), then continued along the track towards Cwm Llwch Farm, now less that 500 metres away. I believe the fact that the track curves out of sight is significant, for when Tommy became frightened only a short way along this track, he was already out of sight of the bridges. Having decided to return to his father, Tommy came running back down the track, crossed the first bridge, but then lost his sense of direction and missed the turning across the second bridge, instead turning left along a path (long disappeared) leading towards the rifle range. Bear in mind that, at the turn of the century, the area was far more heavily wooded, and the Login camp would have been out of sight.

Retrace your steps for a short distance to reach a level area with a high embankment to the left. Bear left on to the track that climbs the embankment, then cross the field alongside the right edge of the wood to reach a fence close to a stile. Do not cross the stile, but turn left into the wood on a faint and muddy track, and follow this until a gate on the right gives access to the open hillside.

Directly beyond the gate, a wide, grassy path heads slightly uphill towards the looming bulk of Pen Milan. Follow this and its slightly muddier continuation through clumps of gorse to reach a more open, flatter area where you should trend right, heading directly towards the steepening hillside, eventually coming to a rough path – an old quarry track. Tommy would most likely have reached this area having followed the path used by the soldiers to travel between the Login and the rifle

*Retrospective view down the quarry track on Pen Milan. Tommy almost certainly followed this track in his search for his Grandparents' farmhouse.*

range. Follow the quarry track to the left, climbing gently, soon reaching a shallow cutting overgrown with clumps of gorse, which leads to the lowest of two zigzag bends – a fine viewpoint where the whole of Cwm Llwch is laid out in front of you. Continue along the track, more steeply now as it swings back to the right, the views increasing all the time, then swing back left at the top zigzag, soon emerging from the cutting as the track becomes a shelf across the mountainside. In front and to the right are the remains of extensive tilestone quarries – the rocks here break easily and naturally into slabs, and were quarried for roofing tiles and flagstones. These quarries were in use at the turn of the century and the track would have been very well-defined – a semblance of industrial normality for a five-year-old from the industrial valleys.

Continue along the quarry track, climbing more gently now, eventually reaching the top of the spur where the views open out to the west (right). As you leave the tilestone quarries behind, the track becomes less well defined, but the onward route is still obvious, eventually heading straight towards the flat summit in the distance (Corn Du). At a point where you can see almost the entire route to the summit, trend left towards the

*RIGHT* The Tommy Jones obelisk, looking west. This picture was taken in 1984, since when the obelisk has been moved a few metres to a point overlooking Llyn Cwm Llwch.

*BELOW* Llyn Cwm Llwch from the summit of Corn Du. The Tommy Jones obelisk is situated at the top of the shadowy area to the left of the lake. Tommy must have walked the entire length of the ridge beyond, starting along the quarry track, just visible at the top of the paler-coloured slopes.

edge of the steep drops, and a short distance further on you will come to a large granite obelisk – the Tommy Jones Memorial – marking the spot at which Tommy's body was found.

From here you have a choice of routes. If time is tight, weather is threatening, or body is flagging, you can descend to Llyn Cwm Llwch – the mountain lake below. The way is obvious – simply turn so that the steep slopes are to your right, and follow the narrow but well-trodden path it as is curves around the headwall and descends. Bear right at the fork, and zigzag steeply down to the shores of the lonely and picturesque lake . . . an ideal place for a brew! Alternatively, it is not much further to the summit of Corn Du, and only a stone's throw from there to Pen y Fan, the highest mountain in southern Britain. Again, the route to the tops is obvious – simply continue up the well-defined path with steep drops to the left, eventually reaching a pitched stone path leading up the ridge to the flat-topped summit of Corn Du. Having come this far, it would be a shame to ignore the real top, so cross the summit in an easterly direction, descend to the saddle, and follow the well-trodden highway of a path to the summit of Pen y Fan.

The geology here is visibly interesting. The whole, vast area is composed of parallel layers of rock which descend gently towards the south, soon to disappear beneath younger limestones, and eventually under the South Wales coal-basin. The resulting 'dip slope' is nowhere more noticeable than from here. The more recent of these rocks were laid down under an ancient sea, and it is a sobering thought that the summit rocks of Pen y Fan, currently at a respectable 886 metres above sea level, were once part of a tidal beach. The proof is all around you: look for the ripple-marks in the slabs of rock on the summit. What you are seeing is a fossilised, sandy sea shore.

To the north, the sandwich of rocks has been broken, resulting in the steep, north-facing escarpment which is one of the great landscape features of the Brecon Beacons National Park. The north-east face of Pen y Fan, a 300-metre precipice of loose gullies, broken grass ledges and tottering sandstone capped by a vertical headwall, is a superb example. Far too loose and broken for rock climbing, it does, however, provide some interesting winter routes, but rarely comes into condition nowadays.

While you could retrace your steps to the obelisk and descend to the lake, there is a more direct descent, though I have known people turn ashen at the prospect. It is not a route for the unwary, nor one that should be attempted without the required equipment and technical skills in winter conditions. The route starts down the steep, loose north ridge. While this is simple enough to locate in good visibility, you would be wise to keep well to the left, away from the headwall, when trying to find the correct route in misty conditions. Once located, scramble carefully down the loose path, with increasingly good views to the right, across the north-east face of Pen y Fan. Where the angle eases to an almost level shoulder, just after another path cuts left and back to the saddle between Pen y Fan and Corn Du, turn hard left and start to descend the pathless and sometimes very steep hillside, heading directly towards the lake. The angle soon eases, but the final approach is blocked by a nasty boggy area – avoid this to the left, and follow the right side of the shallow valley beyond.

Llyn Cwm Llwch is a tranquil pool trapped behind a wall of debris

left behind when the ice and snow of the last ice age finally melted. It is an atmospheric spot (especially if you are lucky enough to be here alone) – a place of legends. For a start, it is supposedly bottomless – and local stories tell that if all the bell ropes from Llanfaes Church (in Brecon) were tied end-to-end, they would not reach the bottom. According to several sources, there is a secret fairy door by the shores of the lake that once opened each May Day so that we, mere mortals, could

*Pen y Fan from Corn Du.*

visit Fairyland. Access was freely given until, one day, an ungracious visitor stole a flower from a fairy, and brought it back to the real world. Since that time, no mortal has been able to find any sign of the fairy door. Moreover, another common story tells that, some years after the fairy door was closed, a group of people from Brecon decided to drain the lake in order to find the fairy treasure that was undoubtedly buried there. They cut a trench through the moraine dam, and as the water level began to drop, an island appeared in the middle of the lake, upon which was a bearded giant in a flowing white gown. He spoke to them (in Welsh) in a booming voice, and told them to go away and leave him in peace. 'If anyone disturbs my peace again, I will cause the waters of the lake to rise up and flood the town of Brecon'.

Having been refreshed, leave the lake via the outflow and descend, steeply at first, on a well-defined path which leads to a low cairn where you merge with the direct path from the Tommy Jones obelisk. Straight ahead, the main path leads directly to a stile in the hill fence, but a more interesting route takes the fainter path that heads slightly left across the tussocky grass, soon descending across steep slopes to the left. Head towards three obvious and very ancient stones on a slight platform, then continue on the faint path over a slight rise to reach four substantial if rusty iron structures. This is where the targets for the army range

*Cribyn from Pen y Fan. The conical summit of Sugar Loaf is just visible in the far distance.*

*Pen y Fan and Corn Du from near the ancient stones above the old army targets.*

were situated, and the iron boxes are the shelters behind which sat the people who moved the targets – probably a job given as a punishment! Some of the targets moved up and down, while others moved from side to side, and there are the scant remains of the tracks and various mechanisms strewn about the place. Firing positions (butts) were situated along the floor of the valley at 100-yard intervals for a distance of half a mile, but there is now little evidence of these, and the furthest ones have disappeared altogether. When you have finished exploring, walk past the rightmost (eastern) box, and continue straight across the hillside towards the top end of the fence, just beyond which you regain the main path at the hill-fence stile and a National Trust marker stone.

Climb the stile and continue down the well-trodden but grassy path, soon entering a wooded section where the path becomes a track, eventually emerging just above a low, white building. This is Cwm Llwch farmhouse, where Tommy's grandparents once lived, now used as a mountain hut

*View north from the National Trust marker stone in Cwm Llwch.*
*Cwm Llwch farmhouse is a short distance into the mist.*

for walking groups and suchlike. Pass to the left of the building and the farm yard by crossing the two obvious stiles, then follow the stone wall on the right to rejoin the track on the far side. As you follow the track down the valley, consider the fact that Willie John ran this way to warn Tommy's grandmother of the imminent arrival of guests, then ran back to the Login. You are now following in Willie John's footsteps, and you will arrive at the footbridge by the Login in a matter of minutes – so short a time for such a huge tragedy to start to unfold.

It is but a simple matter to cross the footbridge and retrace your earlier steps to the car park.

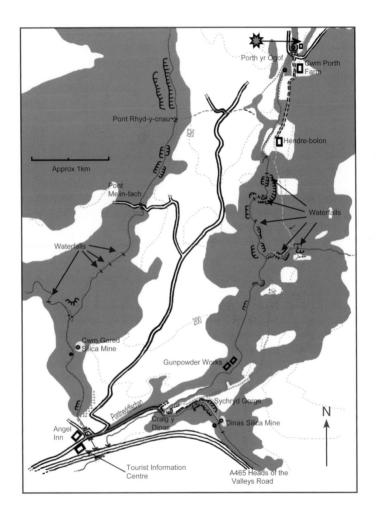

Porth yr Ogof

Cwm Porth
Farm

Pont Rhyd-y-cnau

Hendre-bolon

Approx 1km

Pont
Melin-fach

Waterfalls

Waterfalls

Cwm Gored
Silica Mine

Gunpowder Works

Pontneddfechan

Sychryd Gorge

Craig y
Dinas

Dinas Silica Mine

N

Angel
Inn

Tourist Information
Centre

A465 Heads of the
Valleys Road

# 5.
# GUNPOWDER, SILICA AND LIMESTONE

*A wonderful wooded waterside walk involving Merlin's misplaced magic, deep gorges, spectacular waterfalls, and forgotten industry, all hidden along the heads of the South Wales valleys.*

## BACKGROUND INFORMATION

**Location** The 'waterfall country' in the central southern part of the Brecon Beacons National Park.

**Start & finish point** Cwm Porth car park at SN928124 (marked on OS maps), near Ystradfellte, a small village north of Pontneddfechan.

**Maps needed** OS Explorer OL12.

**Map distance** 15 kilometres.

**Height gain** 350 metres.

**Terrain** Good paths for the most part, although some are exposed and cross very steep slopes, while others are rocky. Parts of the walk are often muddy.

**Duration** Allow 5 hours.

**Hazards** Steep slopes and large drops; slippery rocks and fast flowing water. The optional visit to the cascades below Sgwd Eira involves a short section of scrambling on loose slopes.

**Public transport** The nearest bus routes are at Penderyn and Pontneddfechan. The nearest railway station is at Merthyr Tydfil.

**Amenities/facilities** The car park (pay & display) has a part-time warden, excellent information boards, a small shop, picnic area and public toilets. There is a public house (The New Inn) in Ystradfellte. In summer there is often an ice cream van where the lane leaves the main road.

I AM NOT, AND HAVE NEVER BEEN, particularly politically correct! I tend to speak my mind, to tell it as it is (or, at least, as I see it), which has got me into trouble on more than one occasion. I dislike the sycophantic politeness of politics, the glossy half-truths of diplomacy, the meaningless psychobabble that so often passes for informed discussion. And as for the Nanny State – what a travesty that is! The search to eliminate all risk is little more than a journey towards sterility, and I am convinced that it is at least partly responsible for the headlong rush to worship the false god that is litigation.

Don't get me wrong: I have nothing against safety, nor against warning about potential danger and seeking to reduce risk – but it has all gone too far. People should take responsibility for their own actions, their own accidents, rather than seeking to lay the blame at other people's feet. You go too near the edge of a cliff and fall over . . . You go swimming in a wild river and get swept away . . . You walk through woodland in a gale and get hit by a falling branch . . . How can any of these possibly be anyone else's fault but your own? Unless, of course, you have been told to do so. But being told *not* to do so is *not* the answer, for it does nothing to make you face up to your responsibilities. Moreover, this meddlesome mollycoddling has several other consequences, many of which are well-illustrated by this walk. The sad fact is that, despite its magic (and you only have to walk here to feel it), this area is littered with the knee-jerk directives and consequences of the Nanny State!

Although well hidden and nowhere near the beaten track, Cwm Porth car park at the start of this walk is exceptionally popular. Indeed, it is not unusual for it to be full during sunny summer weekends. The easiest approach is from the A4059, which links Hirwaun (on the A465 Heads of the Valleys road) with the A470 – the main road between Merthyr Tydfil and Brecon. A couple of kilometres north of Penderyn, a narrow lane bears off towards the hamlet of Ystradfellte. Follow this lane and turn left at every opportunity (ignoring farm tracks and a car park), the final turn (towards the end of the forestry) being sudden and unexpected. The car park is on the right at the bottom of the hill.

How things have changed in the forty years that I have known this place! When I first came here in the late 1960s, there was hardly any development at all. By the mid-1980s, however, when I used to visit on a regular basis, the car park and toilets had been built, and the signage and crowds had started to multiply. For such an out-of-the-way place, it became extraordinarily popular (which speaks volumes for the quality of the local landscape), but disliking the crowds and the signs which told me what I should and should not do, I forsook the area in search of quieter wilderness to explore. Little has changed in the intervening years – except that the development has continued! The car park, once small and rough,

is now large, surfaced, and pay-and-display, while the former iconic but totally out-of-place grass roofed hut has been replaced by a modern monstrosity housing an information area, a warden's room and a small shop with a wood-burning stove! To be fair, the building is 100 per cent sustainable, with a wind turbine and photovoltaic roof generating all its electrical needs, but – to my eyes at least – it just doesn't look right! Away from the car park, the main paths are wider while the less well-trodden ones are more overgrown, and much of the original wooden signage has disappeared, only to be replaced by overtly glaring plastic. I do not blame the National Park or Forest Enterprise – they are simply responding to the demands of the Nanny State (although it has to be said that some of the responses are fairly extreme).

It is rare for the car park to be empty of minibuses, yet the reason for their presence is hidden from view, despite its proximity. The information boards and safety notices should give you a clue, particularly those midway along the car park, for they describe Porth yr Ogof, a jewel of a cave that lies directly beneath your feet. Intensely popular with local (and not so local) outdoor education centres, there is seldom a day that goes by without there being at least one group visit (hence the changing areas next to the toilets). Before leaving on the walk proper, it is worth taking a few moments to see what all the fuss is about.

From the gate and stiles behind the caving information boards, follow the obvious path steeply down into the valley over worn and slippery rocks, to reach the bed of the River Mellte. I say 'bed' because there is no guarantee that there will be much water here, most of it having sunk underground some distance upstream. However, 'Mellte' means 'lightning', and the river is aptly named. Just one rainstorm on the nearby mountains, and the water comes rushing in a flood pulse – a sudden surge that can transform the rocky bed into a torrent of turbulence within a matter of minutes. Ignoring the signs, one of which tells you that you are entering a hard hat area (!), another of which warns you to 'beware of falling rocks from above' (From which other direction would they fall?), turn right at the bottom of the descent path, pass a wooden bench dedicated to the memory of Paul Esser (a caver diver who died here in 1971), and continue around to the right, the sound of rushing water beckoning you on, even on a dry day. A few paces further and you will discover that the sound comes from a hole at the base of the cliff, where a tumbling torrent briefly sees daylight before plunging into darkness again. This is Tradesman's Entrance, one of fifteen entrances into the Porth yr Ogof cave system. Upstream, the passage is only accessible to cave divers; downstream, however, it can be followed into the main part of the cave.

The apparently quarried face above the cave is the result of an attempt, several years ago, to remove some loose rocks and make the area safe. The National Park and Forestry Commission Wales closed the entrance for several weeks while they carried out 'remedial work'. But you cannot tame nature – a few months after the area had been 'stabilised', several large rocks moved making access to the upstream parts of the cave more problematic than usual.

Retrace your steps to the bottom of the descent route and continue straight ahead over the stile. Bear left over the rocks, and gaze in awe at the largest cave entrance in Wales, some 17.5m wide and 5m high. Closer inspection is highly recommended. The main way on into the inner reaches of the cave is along a large passage to the right, just inside the cave mouth,

*The impressive main entrance of Porth yr Ogof*
*– the largest cave mouth in Wales.*

and should only be entered by correctly equipped, experienced or well-led cavers. However, on a fine, dry day it is possible to walk straight ahead along the main passage for some distance without the need for additional light, although it may be necessary to scramble around huge branches (and even whole trees) that have been washed into the cave during times of flood – a sobering thought! As your eyes get used to the dark, keep a look out for fossils in the rock, and for several smaller passages leading off on either side. Eventually you reach an impasse at a deep pool, on the far side of which a patch of white calcite (the mineral of limestone) resembles a horse's head. This is the White Horse Pool (indeed, the cave was once known as White Horse Cave).

According to legend, back in the Dark Ages, there lived in the region a beautiful princess who rode around on a great, white stallion. One day she was riding through the valley when she was set upon by a band of brigands. Fearing for her life and modesty, she rode into the cave, hoping against hope that someone would save her. The Dark Ages were, of course, Arthurian times, and Merlin, sensing that something was afoot,

*The infamous Porth yr Ogof resurgence pool, where the Afon Melite emerges into daylight. Although it looks idyllic, this is a frighteningly dangerous spot.*

picked up the princess's cry for help. Watching events unfold in his crystal ball, he realised that a successful outcome demanded instant action, so he ordered the river to rise up in flood and sweep away the brigands. Unfortunately, Merlin was not the most accomplished of wizards, and he neglected to think his actions through to their logical conclusion. Yes, the brigands were all swept away and drowned – but the princess and her white charger were also in the path of the flood! So upset was Merlin that his actions had caused the death of both the princess and her horse, that he caused their images to be forever graven on the rocks where they died. The horse drowned in the pool, hence the image on the far wall – the princess drowned in a chamber deep inside the cave where there is a stalagmite that resembles a fair maiden.

Retrace your steps to the car park, walk past the shop to the entrance, cross the lane diagonally to the left and take the first path to the right, which crosses an embankment. A fenced area below and to the right of the embankment guards a pothole leading into the cave, and there are two more vertical entrances hidden among the boulders on the opposite side of the embankment. A short distance beyond the embankment, you reach a fence where you should ignore the main path and go, instead, through the gate marked 'access for cavers'. You are now walking (sometimes muddily) along what used to be the bed of the river before it disappeared underground, but the water is now flowing (literally) beneath your feet, as will shortly become obvious, for you are soon forced to scramble steeply down into a depression where there are two fenced entrances, both full of rushing water and warning signs. Go thought the corridor between the entrances and continue along the muddy path for a short distance to reach a junction where rocks on the right lead down to a platform above the river. Scramble down carefully. There are three more entrances here – a tiny hole immediately left of the descent route, a more obvious and larger low slot further on and to the left, and the Resurgence Pool itself, where the Mellte emerges into daylight.

I did consider, on a recent visit, that the National Park were doing a good job by removing some of the old wooden warning signs around the cave. Unfortunately, they have replaced them with glaring plastic ones such as you would find on a building site, which is actually a depressingly retrograde step! However, some form of signage is absolutely necessary at this point, for this pool is lethal. Indeed, more that ten people have met their deaths here in the past twenty years, giving the pool an infamous reputation. The problem is that from inside the cave the pool looks calm and inviting as an exit, especially when the sun glints on the water. But there are hugely powerful undercurrents which suck the unwary caver under a wide shelf where the passage is choked with dead branches and other snagging obstructions. If you come here when the river levels are low, you can actually see the water bubbling up from narrow slots underneath the platform on which you are standing. This is not the place to go swimming.

Having wondered at so many deaths in such an apparently benign and tranquil place, scramble back to the path, turn right and climb past more signs to join a wider track. Follow this to the right, soon reaching a riverside meadow (unfortunately full of noise and lager cans on summer weekends). Turn left, and make your way on to a path alongside the river, a pleasant (and much quieter) route that you follow for some distance.

Shortly after a wooded section (gated at either end), you reach a footbridge across the river where there are more warning signs. Do not cross the bridge, but continue straight ahead to climb a short, rocky section, then veer left and up again. Do not be tempted to follow the riverside path – keep left and keep climbing – eventually walking uphill to the right of a wooden fence. At the top, follow the path to the right, soon reaching another wooden fence guarding the top of the steep slopes to your right. Continue with the sound of rushing water getting louder all the time, eventually descending steeply between fences, past a sign warning of cliffs, to reach a fine viewpoint overlooking the first of many waterfalls – Sgwd Clun-gwyn. Paradoxically, the fence ends at what is potentially the most dangerous point – where people spend more time looking through the viewfinders of their cameras, and less time looking where they are putting their feet or how close they are to the edge.

Having gazed your fill, turn your back on the falls and continue along the path that runs along the left side of the gorge. Although wide and well trodden at the start, the path soon narrows as it crosses increasingly steep slopes, then curves to the right below a high bluff, following a wide bend in the river. This is not the place to let children run on ahead! After more warning signs, and just beyond the second of two blind left-hand

*The fenced corridor guarding the approach to Sgwd Clun-gwyn, the first of many waterfalls.*

bends, the path follows a narrow ledge across a cliff, high above another waterfall, the exposure growing dramatically as the drop suddenly increases by the depth of the fall. Just beyond this, where the path splits, veer right and start to descend, soon reaching a very steep, loose and awkward section leading down a rocky spur. Several paths lead off to the right of this descent route, some at half height, several towards the bottom, all of which give access to superb viewpoints of the various levels of a complex series of falls – Sgwd Isaf Clun-gwyn.

From the bottom of the lowest set of falls, continue along the left bank of the river following a path that is remarkable for its mud. Strangely, the least muddy option seems to be to get as close to the river as possible. Approach quietly and you may well see rare dippers along this section – small, bobbing birds recognisable by their white chest feathers and kamikaze antics in the fast flowing water. It is only a short distance to the next waterfall – Sgwd y Pannwr – which starts as a vertical cleft parallel to, and in the middle of, the stream bed. There is an excellent viewpoint overlooking the plunge pool, just beyond the tree, from where, if you are

*RIGHT* Beyond the barriers at Sgwd Clun-gwyn. Note how close to the edge one has to be to take a picture!

*BELOW* The lower section of Sgwd Isaf Clun-gwyn, a complex series of waterfalls and cascades in one of the deepest parts of the Mellte Gorge.

LEFT *Sgwd y Pannwr. Dippers often fly in and out of the cascades, almost as if they are playing with the water.*

RIGHT *Part of the complex of cascades known as Sgwd Isaf Cilhepste, in the Hepste Gorge, downstream of Sgwd yr Eira, and well off the beaten track.*

lucky, you might witness the dippers flying into the waterfall, almost as if they are playing with the torrent. Continue around to the left of the plunge pool, but ignore the main track, instead turning right on to a narrow, sometimes overgrown path that almost immediately bears left across an awkward boulder field, beyond which it becomes easier as it climbs through the woods. Keep to the left throughout this section (unless you want to descend to river level just downstream of the falls, where a rock platform makes a pleasant refreshments spot).

The path through the woods becomes muddy and overgrown, and then steepens dramatically before swinging right and levelling out as it reaches the top of the gorge. Ignoring the many smaller side turnings, continue on the main path, meandering through young silver birch and other older trees, never far away from (and sometimes very close to) the steep slopes to your right. Eventually the path swings left, widens, and begins to descend quite steeply. Towards the bottom of this section, just before it starts to level out, the path splits, the less well-defined right-hand branch offering an interesting alternative route for the adventurous (described below). The main route, however, continues straight on along a rocky path, soon reaching the river again. I have come across people here wearing puzzled expressions, because the stream appears to be flowing in the wrong direction! This is because you have just crossed a watershed and are now walking upstream along the Afon Hepste as opposed to downstream along the Afon Mellte! Follow the path upstream, and the spectacular Sgwd yr Eira is only a short distance further.

The more adventurous might like to follow a slightly more circuitous route. From the junction on the descent path, follow the less well-defined path to the right, descending past barriers of brushwood (apparently placed to deter visitors – even though this is access land) then continuing along a more obvious path to reach the river near a small glade. Turn left and follow a faint path upstream to the entrance of a narrow gorge, and scramble up on the left to reach a fine viewpoint overlooking the lowest in a series of cascades collectively known as Sgwd Isaf Cilhepste – Lower Cilhepste

*Approaching Sgwd yr Eira. Even in the depths of the gorge, the warning signs keep on appearing.*

Falls. Above and to the left is an obvious rocky bluff. Gain the base of this by carefully ascending the very steep bank, then scramble up the bluff – the easiest route being to the left. Once at the top, continue along the left edge of the gorge on a very narrow path above intimidating drops, the river rising to meet you. Sgwd yr Eira is just beyond the far end of the gorge.

Sgwd yr Eira (Falls of Snow) is a gem of a waterfall, a major attraction being that you can walk behind it. Indeed, this is the most convenient way to cross the river hereabouts. Believe it or not, it has been negotiated (on purpose) by canoe – a trip (or plummet!) that featured on the BBC's *Blue Peter*, and led to an entry in the Guinness Book of Records as it was (at the time) a new world record drop of 15.8 metres. In May 2007, following the discovery of loose rocks above the falls, the footpath leading to the waterfall and the fall itself were fenced off 'in the interests of visitor safety'. There were then 'talks and investigations' involving the National Park Authority, Forestry Commission Wales and the Countryside Council for Wales, in an attempt to agree a way forward. The talking continued for over a year, during which time 'Path Prohibition Orders'

*Sgwd yr Eira.*

were posted at all the major access points, and tape barriers erected at either end of the main path leading to the falls. But when I arrived to do some basic research for this book, nowhere could I find any explanation of why the path had been closed, and I still managed to get to the falls using good paths, and without crossing any barriers.

While I have no issue with the need for public safety, there seems to be a double standard at work here. Firstly, there was no obvious information available on site to tell the public why the restrictions were there, which meant that many people ignored the barriers and continued to walk behind the falls, unaware of the potential risk. Secondly, I find it difficult to reconcile the closure of Sgwd Eira because of potentially unstable, overhanging rocks, with the fence at Sgwd Clun-gwyn that stops short of the most dangerous area so that people can get as close as possible to the unstable, overhanging edge of a large vertical drop in order to take the best photo. Last, but by no means least, when similar problems occurred at the Tradesman's Entrance to Porth yr Ogof, rocks still fell despite the remedial works. The bottom line, surely, is that such things as loose rock are part of a natural process that will continue until the end of time – with or without human intervention.

The footpaths and the waterfall are now open again, and yet more signs have been installed on the approach paths to either side, these ones warning of the dangers posed by slippery paths and falling rocks. They also inform you that if – despite the dire warnings – you decide to follow the path behind the waterfall, you do so at your own risk, and they suggest that you should not hang about below the cliffs, but continue away from the waterfall until you reach safer ground. Giving people the relevant information and telling them that they should take responsibility for their own actions . . . ? It would seem that sense has, at last, prevailed!

You can, if you wish, return to the start direct from Sgwd yr Eira, thus significantly shortening the walk. To do this, climb the steep stepped path that negotiates the northern side of the gorge (the side on which you arrived), just downstream of Sgwd yr Eira, turn right at the top, and follow the path which soon turns left and climbs through the woods. On reaching the forestry track, turn left and follow this for some distance, keeping straight on at all junctions, eventually reaching a gate, after which you pass to the left of buildings at Hendre-bolon. Continue along the track beyond, eventually arriving at Cwm Porth farm. Cross a stile on the left to gain a continuation of the track, which leads almost immediately to the lane adjacent to the car park entrance.

Walking behind the waterfall is an exhilarating experience at any time, but especially if the Hepste is in spate. Put on your waterproofs, then follow a rough path along the left bank of the river, soon climbing slightly to gain an obvious ledge. I know it looks unlikely, but the ledge continues behind the waterfall and emerges on the far side, and offers a simple if somewhat slippery route to the far side of the stream. In low water conditions it is just possible to do the whole journey without getting wet, but most of the time you will get wet from the spray, and when the stream is high you will get soaked because huge amounts of spray are sucked back into the passage behind the waterfall by the vacuum caused by the fast-moving water. No matter what the water conditions, however, only a few people can make the crossing without breaking into a huge grin. This is due, I am led to believe, to the positive ions caused by the moving water, which cause the body to produce adrenaline and noradrenalin, which in turn produce short-term euphoria!

Having passed behind the waterfall, follow the obvious path that climbs steeply out of the gorge, loose and rocky to start, then zigzagging slightly more easily up stupidly high, wooden steps (they had to be high because of the angle of the slope), eventually reaching the top of the gorge by a large, low boulder – the perfect place to stop for a few moments and recover from the ascent. Once your pulse is back to normal, follow a horribly muddy path to the right (the nearby finger post indicates that you are heading towards Craig y Dinas), soon reaching a narrower and less muddy section, traversing across the very steep, wooded slopes of the Hepste Gorge. Continue on this path for some distance, trending generally downhill through patches of modern forestry interspersed with ancient woodland, eventually passing the scant remains of a long abandoned farmstead, Cilhepste-cerig, on your left, and eventually emerging from the conifers into an area of young silver birch, where the views open out dramatically. To the right is the wooded gorge of the Afon Mellte, beyond which the Heads of the Valleys road snakes its way through the Vale of Neath, the noise reaching you even at this distance. The path deteriorates as it plunges back into conifers, soon descending steeply to a gate, beyond which it becomes little better than a stream. It

*One of the many entrances to the Dinas Silica Mine at the top of the Sychryd Gorge.*

is, however, a simple enough matter to continue with dry feet, and the wetness only lasts a short distance, only to be replaced (in winter) by mud, and (in summer) by high walls of bracken to either side.

Your path lies along a bracken-covered ridge, separated from a rocky escarpment to your left by a shallow valley, and the noise of distant traffic is soon replaced by the roar of rapids in the Mellte Gorge, below and to your right. Just beyond a short, steep, rocky descent to the right, you reach a finger post decorated with a cannon – the waymark for a local heritage trail visiting the Glyn-neath Gunpowder Works (more of which anon). Continue straight ahead, soon reaching a T-junction with a grassy track, with a wire fence beyond. Although your onward path is to the right, a slight detour will take you to the Dinas Silica Mine and the spectacular Sychryd Gorge, so turn left and follow the track around the corner, immediately bearing right on to a scrappy path that leads steeply down to a terrace above the river. The several entrances to the Dinas Silica Mine are partially hidden in the cliffs behind and to your left, and a further entrance is obvious at the far side of the bridge across the river.

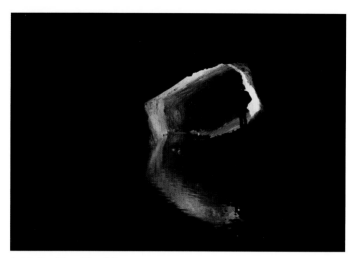

*Inside the Dinas Silica Mine.*

The rock hereabouts contains bands of quartzite – a hard rock containing a high percentage of silica (silicon oxide), which gives it an extremely high melting point – and silica was mined here from the late eighteenth century until as recently as 1964. The heyday began when William Weston Young developed a method of producing high quality firebricks from the rock, the so-called 'Dinas Bricks' being manufactured at the nearby Pont Walby brickworks, and used to line the furnaces of the local ironworks. So successful were they, that they were soon exported all over the world. Even today, the Russian word for 'firebrick' is 'dinas'!

To visit the gorge, walk downstream following the obvious path to the right of the river, taking great care as the path is not in the best state of repair. You are re-entering the world of signs, prohibitions, and corporate risk aversion, and barriers are often put here in an attempt to prevent access. Despite the fact that the path is a right of way and the area is Access Land, it would, of course, be irresponsible of me to encourage you to cross any barrier. However, if you were to follow it, you would find that the path leads directly into the magnificent Sychryd Gorge with its huge overhang, the cliffs above giving some of the best natural limestone rock climbing in South Wales. At the far end, the Sychryd stream drops to the valley floor in a series of steep cascades, a narrow ledge across the cliff now gated to prevent people using it as a hair-raising descent route. Various pieces of rusting iron are all that remain of a ramp that once provided access to the Silica Mines.

Retrace your steps to the T-junction above the mines, and follow the grassy track with the fence to your left, soon trending away from the fence and then dropping steeply (and carefully) down a rocky incline, a cliff rising to your left and big drops to your right. There have been recent landslides towards the bottom of this incline, so caution is advised. At the bottom, you reach Craig y Dinas, an impressive vertical rock face with a large slab beyond. If you come here in summer, you will almost certainly find the car park full of minibuses and the slabs thronged with rock climbers, for this area is beloved of outdoor pursuits centres. The track to the left at the far end of the car park (blocked by a boulder to

*The spectacular Sychryd Gorge. The old miners track is obvious along the base of the cliff, and the start of the huge overhang is just visible slightly below centre.*

prevent vehicle access) leads to Bwa Maen, an impressive arch of rock at the bottom of the cascades falling from the Sychryd Gorge.

It is amazing how fast nature reclaims her own. This particular area is one with which I was entranced in the mid-1980s. I spent countless hours here, climbing the rocks and exploring the caves and mines, wondering about the people who made their living in such scenic surroundings. For a variety of reasons, most of which had to do with increasing popularity, I had not visited Dinas Rock for about ten years when I started to research this book. My memories of the place are not as it is now. Despite its popularity, much has become lost beneath bracken and brambles, and on a recent visit I failed to find what was once a major causeway leading to a mine entrance – it was simply too overgrown! It seems that the current users only visit specific areas.

But it is not only nature that has changed this place almost out of all recognition – man, too, has had a profound effect thanks to safety legislation and risk assessment. Even in the 1980s the writing was on the wall. The ramp that gave easy access to the Sychryd Gorge was demolished because it was considered unsafe, yet it probably cost as much to demolish it as it would have done to refurbish it. Twenty years on, the scars are still there, and people are talking about encouraging tourism – so long, of course, as all the dangers are eliminated! Meanwhile, hordes of 'deprived' children from urban (and not-so-urban) areas boisterously slither – wetsuited, helmeted and roped – up the cascades, then jump from the gorge edge, sometimes extravagantly, often fearfully, into deep pools with names like 'Loony's Leap' and 'The Black Hole'. I have absolutely nothing against the children nor what they are doing – but I do have qualms about the way in which they are doing it. It is all so sanitised, so transparent, so molly-coddlingly regulated. The adventure has been legislated out of Adventure.

As the regulations becomes increasingly complex and time-consuming, so only large businesses can afford to offer such activities, and that brings its own set of problems. While there is much to be said for running outdoor businesses in a professional and businesslike way, problems start to occur if the primary motive is to make money. I take my hat off to those who choose to instruct outdoor activities as a vocation, but I deplore those who use it as an instrument of bravado, as a way to show off, or as a means of trying to make a fast buck. Unfortunately, there appears to be an increase in the latter at the expense of the former.

*Craig y Dinas, much beloved of Outdoor Centres, ringed with fences and warning signs, and with the upper slab covered in wire netting to discourage rock fall.*

Leave the Craig y Dinas car park over the bridge, and follow the road into a housing estate. Immediately to the right, a waymarked track leads to the ruins of the Glyn-neath Gunpowder Works, spread out along the banks of the Afon Mellte for a distance of about 3 kilometres. Gunpowder was made here from 1820 until 1931, with everything sited well away from habitation in case of accident! Being at a remote location, its main source of power was water, and while most of the buildings are in a sorry state of repair (many having been devastated by fire in 1932), many of the weirs are still well preserved. Your onward route, however, lies along the road through the housing estate, past the 30 mph signs. After about 700 metres, you reach a junction with a larger road at The Dinas Inn, where the Heads of the Valleys road can be seen beyond the housing on the left, running along a high bridge. Continue straight on to reach The Angel Inn, which has a welcoming Hikers Bar. There are public toilets here, and an excellent Information Centre opposite the pub, where you can find out more about the gunpowder works, the waterfalls area and the Fforest Fawr Geopark.

Turn right on to a lane to the right of the pub, past a small parking area and a National Park Information board. Directly in front is a

*ABOVE A brick-lined drainage adit beside the old tramroad running alongside the Afon Nedd, one of several seen on the way to Sgwd Gwladys.*

*LEFT Sgwd Gwladys from the tourist viewpoint. Getting closer to this waterfall is possible, but not easy!*

*The route beyond the confluence. The footbridge to the right leads towards the Cwm Gored Silica Mine, but the main route carries straight on, past yet another warning sign.*

large iron gate containing the words 'Sgwd Gwladys'. Go through the kissing gate to its left, and follow an excellent path alongside the Afon Nedd (River Neath), your right ear once again assailed by the sound of rushing water. There are soon low but impressive cliffs to the left (with large overhangs at their base), and not long after, the regular remains of sleeper stones make it obvious that you are travelling along an old tramroad, built to service the silica mines ahead. Indeed, there are many mines hereabouts, including a fenced-off entrance to the left of the path, immediately beyond the second metal gate, another (very wet) entrance, a short distance further, and yet another, just beyond the wooden steps. There are also regular benches and picnic tables, and the local council is to be applauded for trying to make this once industrialised stretch of river more accessible and visitor friendly.

You eventually reach a confluence where there are two footbridges. Your onward path lies over the first footbridge, but it is well worth continuing along the left bank of the stream for a further 250 metres in order to view Sgwd Gwladys, a fine waterfall, believed to be named after one of the twenty-six daughters of Brychan, who was King of Brycheiniog in the fifth century. Retrace your steps to the bridge, cross it and turn right. Another footbridge on the right leads (after 400 metres) to Cwm Gored Silica Mine (worth an exploratory visit if you have the time and inclination), but the main route lies alongside the stream, following a rough path towards Pont Melin-fach, past more signs warning you about cliffs. This path, rough and muddy in places, climbs steadily for some distance, and leads past a series of picturesque waterfalls and cascades, including the aptly named 'Horseshoe Falls'. At each, there is a minor path leading to a good viewpoint. The further you get from habitation, the less well-trodden the path, but it soon begins to improve again as you near Sgwd Ddwli, a short distance beyond which is a popular tourist picnic area and car park at Pont Melin-fach. There are so many falls and cascades along this section of river, that no single photograph can do them justice. I therefore leave the joy of discovery to the walker!

Leave the car park across the bridge and immediately turn left over a waymarked stile. Pont Melin-fach means 'bridge of the small mill', and the ruins of the mill in question lie directly in front of you, the remains of the water supply leat obvious behind it, running parallel to the stream. Although you can follow a very rough path beyond the leat, this is impassable after wet weather and is often obstructed by deadfall, so the best route lies up and to the right, immediately beyond the stile, the path soon curving left to run along the top of the bank above the stream. While not as good as the paths you have followed thus far, it is still an obvious, stiled route, and offers pleasant walking with good views of the river below. Eventually you reach a finger post, just beyond which is a bridge – Pont Rhyd-y-cnau – where you turn right on to a very loose and rocky track that zigzags steeply up the side of the gorge. Follow this to a lane and turn right, climbing to the top of the watershed between the Afon Nedd (alongside which you have just been walking) and the Afon Mellte (alongside which you walked at the start), with expansive views towards the top. You soon reach a T-junction with a wider lane. Turn left and then almost immediately bear right through a gate on to a bridleway signposted to Porth yr Ogof, heading gently downhill into the valley of the Mellte.

*One of many cascades along the Afon Nedd between the confluence and Pont Melin-fach. This one is near the aptly names Horseshoe Falls.*

Just after a tree-lined section, veer left through a well-waymarked bridle gate into a muddy cutting, the path shared with a stream in very wet weather! Pass to the right of an old barn and go through another gate, cross a ford (there is a footbridge!), and enter a rocky cutting, which can be overgrown in summer. Continue straight ahead (ignoring turnings into fields to either side) to reach yet another bridle gate, then start to descend on a better path. The car park at Cwm Porth is a short distance further, through more gates.

## Footnote

As I write this (September 2008), Wales (and the Midlands and North East England) are reeling from the effects of storms. The flooding is on a similar scale to the previous year – an event we were warned would become more common. But no one expected it to happen again within fourteen months.

There is a connection between these events and the previous paragraphs! Increasingly extreme weather patterns will have a cumulative effect on the landscape, and if we are to continue to have the freedom to roam that we currently enjoy, we need to re-evaluate the way we look at 'risk'. If we are being 'prohibited' from following a footpath because there is a slightly increased chance we might get hit by falling rocks, how small a leap is it to forbidding us to walk on the mountains because there is the possibility that we might experience extreme weather? Okay – so I overplay the scenario – but is there not some truth? Has it not already begun?

When we walk in the mountains, we live in an environment of risk. Wind blows, sun shines, snow submits to gravity and avalanches, and mountains deteriorate – their very being eroded by the atmosphere in which we survive. Rocks will fall, caves will flood, but people will always accept the challenge of risk and achieve wonders. In trying to negate the risk by preventing the public from experiencing it, we alter the human experience.

But isn't any legislation pointless anyway? Despite all the pompous, empire-building debate, the politically correct rules are virtually worthless for, as has already been proved at Sgwd yr Eira, people have scant regard for 'Footpath Prohibition Laws'.

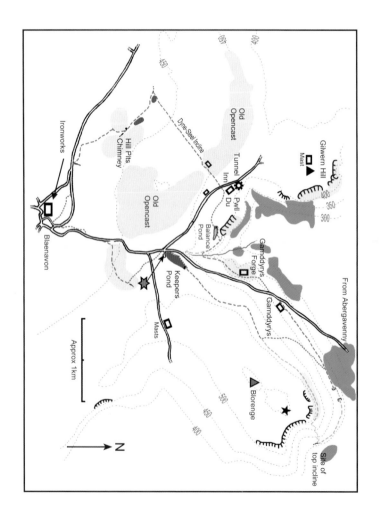

Approx 1km

N

Ironworks

Blaenavon

Hill Pits Chimney

Old Opencast

Dyne-Steel Incline

Old Opencast

Tunnel

Pwll Du Inn

Balance Pond

Keepers Pond

Masts

Garnddyrys Forge

Garnddyrys

From Abergavenny

Gilwern Hill

Mast

Blorenge

Site of top incline

400

450

450

400

350

300

380

450

400

# 6.
# THROUGH THE IRON BARONS' REALM

A surprisingly scenic stroll through a fascinating industrial landscape made famous by the novels of Alexander Cordell, demonstrating how a once-ravaged land can quickly be reclaimed by nature. Cordell fans will recognise many of the place names, and the walk passes several sites mentioned in his books.

## BACKGROUND INFORMATION

**Location** The hills to the north of Blaenavon, a World Heritage Site at the south-eastern edge of the Brecon Beacons National Park.

**Start & finish point** Car Park at Pen-ffordd Goch Pond (known locally as the Keepers Pond) at SO254107, on the B4246 between Blaenavon and Abergavenny.

**Maps needed** OS Explorer OL13.

**Map distance** 15 kilometres.

**Height gain** 100 metres.

If desired, the route can be conveniently divided into two separate walks, of 5 kilometres and 10 kilometres respectively. Details are given in the route description.

**Terrain** Mostly good paths and tracks, although some can be muddy after wet weather.

**Duration** Allow 4 hours.

**Hazards** The optional alternative route on the Blorenge involves an extremely steep descent. Watch out for speeding trials bikes in and around the coal tips!

**Public transport** There are good bus services at Abergavenny and Blaenavon. The nearest railway station is at Abergavenny.

**Amenities/facilities** Abergavenny has all the facilities you would expect from a large town. Blaenavon is a World Heritage Site with many information and tourist amenities, including the excellent Big Pit Mining Museum, Blaenavon Ironworks, and the Pontypool & Blaenavon Railway.

IN THE MID-EIGHTEENTH CENTURY, a small farming village nestling among green fields at the northern end of the Taff Valley became the focus of attention of a new brand of entrepreneur – the 'ironmaster'. Extensive local deposits of iron ore, coal and limestone meant that all the necessary materials for iron making were on hand. The first forges were opened there in 1759, and these were so successful that by 1784 there were four huge ironworks within a 2-mile radius of the village. By the start of the nineteenth century, a mere forty years later, the population of the 'village' of Merthyr Tydfil had increased from less than 200 to over 8,000, making it the largest town in Wales, and this phenomenal growth not only continued, but also accelerated. By 1830, the Dowlais Ironworks were the largest in the world, this one site alone employing almost 9,000 workers, and Merthyr Tydfil – now the largest town in Britain – had gained the title, 'Iron Capital of the World'. Alongside the expansion of the iron industry, there was similar growth in the local coal industry, and by the 1850s this was so profitable that it was cost-effective to export coal to places as far away as India and South America.

Foremost among the early ironmasters were the Crawshays. Originally from Yorkshire, successive generations built a vast iron empire that stretched from Merthyr Tydfil to Blaenavon. This powerful dynasty was founded by Richard Crawshay (1739–1810) who, in his will, split his estate between his son, William, his son-in-law, Benjamin Hall, and his nephew, Joseph Bailey, thus promoting continued expansion. The huge Cyfarthfa ironworks were eventually run by his grandson (also William) who, in 1825 and at a cost of £30,000 – a huge amount of money in those days – built the ostentatious Cyfarthfa Castle where he lived overlooking the unimaginable squalor and misery of his workers' dwellings.

People flocked to the area from all parts of Britain, those skilled in iron-working and coal-mining being offered good housing and high wages. However, huge numbers of unskilled workers were also required, and the conditions in which these labourers lived were nothing short of appalling. Unrest was common. Indeed, following a particularly violent riot in 1816, Joseph Bailey's brother, Crawshay, built a fortified round tower (probably the last private castle to be built in Britain) at the Nantyglo ironworks in order to have a defensible safe haven in which to retreat case of further unrest. As it turned out, this was a wise move, for in 1822, a large group of workers overpowered the local militia and the army was called in to subdue the subsequent riots, the Scots and Greys being stationed in the area for two weeks. Nor was this is end of the unrest. In April 1831, there were major riots in Merthyr Tydfil involving a crowd of several thousand people, and further unrest in June, when twenty-six people were arrested and put on trial – two were sentenced to death, and several others were transported to the penal colony of Australia. Continued political and social unrest culminated in the Chartist uprising of 4 November 1839, when 3,000 people marched on Newport where they were met by an armed response. Several of the marchers were killed, many were injured, and the ringleader, John Frost, and several other men were found guilty of treason and sentenced to be hanged, drawn and quartered – sentences that were later commuted to transportation for life.

Seen through today's eyes, this unrest was not without a degree of justification, for many of the workers were treated little better than slaves. Despite the growing protests, working and housing conditions remained deplorable, and disease was rife. Clean drinking water was a constant problem due not only to the rapid expansion of the population, but also to the fact that the ironmasters diverted most of the streams to supply their steam-engines. Several rivers, including the Taff, effectively became open sewers, and outbreaks of typhoid and cholera were common. By 1848, the mortality rate in Merthyr Tydfil was the third highest in Britain (and the highest in Wales), with over 60 per cent of all burials being of children under the age of five. Despite this, the population continued to soar, and by the middle of the nineteenth century, Merthyr Tydfil was home to over 45,000 people – an increase of more than 44,800 in just a century!

It is, perhaps, telling that Robert Crawshay, Richard's great grandson and the last of the 'Iron Kings', chose to be buried secretly in a quiet village outside Merthyr Tydfil. His body lies beneath a huge slab of rock said to weigh 10 tons, which bears the epitaph, 'God Forgive Me'. No one will ever know whether he actually meant this, or if he was hedging his bets.

I include the preceding paragraphs in an attempt to set the scene for the walk that follows – a walk that takes you through a landscape made famous by Alexander Cordell's book, *Rape of the Fair Country* – a passionate evocation of the struggles of a working family living in the Blaenavon area of early industrial Wales. It is a landscape moulded by the exploitation of iron, of coal and of people – a landscape sculpted and peppered by the

often amazing remains of an industry that once was, but is no more – a landscape that has, at long last, been internationally recognised by being designated a World Heritage Site in recognition of its status as 'one of the finest surviving examples in the world of a landscape created by coal mining and iron making'.

The walk begins at Pen-ffordd-goch Pool (known to locals as Keeper's Pond), a popular beauty spot, much beloved of dog walkers, easily reached along the B4246 from either Abergavenny or Blaenavon. One of three reservoirs built around 1824 to provide water for the nearby Garnddyrys Forge (which you will visit later), the pool is a strange place, set high on the mountain amid a surreal landscape of heather moorland and old waste tips, with spectacular views.

Having read the excellent information board, follow the path around the left side of the pool to a second, equally interesting interpretive display, cross the footbridge, and turn right on to an obvious green path, which you follow for some distance, the views getting more extensive all the time. This old quarry track has none of the foundation stones that characterise the tramroads, which leads me to think it more likely to be a packhorse trail. In addition to admiring the views ahead, keep glancing back and to the left, for you get increasingly good views of Pwll Du Quarry – an important source of limestone for the Blaenavon Ironworks – and above

*The view from the packhorse trail beyond Keepers Pond. The village below is Govilon, to where the people of Pwll Du were relocated in 1963. A large roundabout on the recently rebuilt Heads of the Valleys road is strikingly obvious just left of centre.*

which you can make out the (now dry) reservoir used to provide water for a 'balance lift', the weight of water being used to raise limestone from the quarry floor to the level of the tramroad, which ran across the top section of the quarry. Beyond and slightly right is Gilwern Hill, its surface gouged with more limestone quarries, and beyond, again, are the Black Mountains. Further right, the more modern scar of the Heads of the Valleys road traverses the valley floor, and as you lift your head towards the horizon, you cannot fail to admire Mynydd Pen y Fal (Sugar Loaf), standing in splendid isolation.

Some 1,500 metres beyond Keepers Pond, a much narrower but obvious, waymarked path bears off to the left and heads downhill. Follow this carefully and sometimes muddily down the hillside for a further kilometre to reach a finger post and a well-defined track travelling horizontally around the hillside. This is the line of Hill's Tramroad, more of which anon. Although your onward route lies back and to the left, it is worth bearing right and following the tramroad for a short distance in order to visit the entrance to a short tunnel. If you wish, you can then follow a good path above the tunnel, rejoining the tramroad on the far side and continuing for another 500 metres to reach the remains of a retaining wall on the right. This marks the site of the top of the first of three inclines that led to the canal at Llanfoist, down which iron from Garnddyrys Forge was transported. To be frank, there is nowadays very little to see here apart from some ruined masonry. Once you have explored, retrace your steps to the western-most entrance to the tunnel.

More adventurous view seekers might like to continue along the top track for another kilometre, at which point it enters an area of disturbed ground. Walk straight ahead into the cutting, then head up to the left to get the best views en route to the far end of the quarry, where there is a flat shelf of unquarried rock. Continue straight on across sheep-cropped turf with the village of Govilon directly below – it was to this village that the inhabitants of Pwll Du (QV) were relocated in 1963. Eventually Abergavenny emerges from behind the hillside in front, and the views get even wider before your path is blocked by a large, steep-sided valley – Cwm Craf. It is here that you must descend. Turn hard left and zigzag your way carefully down extremely steep slopes, heading for the right side of the wood that forms the left side of the valley below – a task made even more difficult when the bracken is high. Take extra care as you near the hill fence as the direct descent is guarded by retaining walls. Once on the obvious level track – the route of Hill's Tramroad – find the retaining walls (on the upslope side), and look for the crumbling remains of masonry on the far side of the fence. Although there is nowadays little to see, these mark the top of the upper of three inclines that led to the canal at Llanfoist. Having explored, walk along the well-preserved, level tramroad (with the hillside rising to your left) to reach the entrance to a tunnel, then follow the obvious path above this to reach the far entrance where you rejoin the main route.

Hill's Tramroad is an amazing feat of engineering. Started in 1812 by Thomas Hill, the enterprising manager of the Blaenavon Ironworks, this primitive, horse-drawn railway not only linked the ironworks with the Brecknock & Abergavenny Canal, but also improved the supply of limestone and iron ore, and allowed easy transport of pig iron from the Blaenavon furnaces to Garnddyrys Forge. The spectacular section between Garnddyrys and Pwll Du traverses steep slopes via a shelf cut into the hillside, as you will soon see. The network included three counter-balanced inclines allowing laden tramcars to descend the steep mountainside to the canal at Llanfoist Wharf, branch lines to the limestone quarries at

*The 'cut-and-shut' tunnel on Hill's Tramroad. The tunnel has recently been designated as an Ancient Monument.*

Pwll Du and Gilwern Hill, and another branch leading to Garnddyrys Forge, where there was a tunnel beneath the slag heaps. The amazing Pwll Du tunnel, which ran under the mountain from Pwll Du to Garn-yr-Erw near Blaenavon, was only fractionally less than 2.5 kilometres in length, making it the longest tunnel of its type in Britain. The tunnel at your current location is a 'cut-and-shut' tunnel – effectively, a cutting with a roof – built to prevent land slip and loose material from the quarries above from blocking the tramroad.

Retrace your steps to the finger post at the bottom of the descent route and continue along the tramroad in a south-westerly direction, with many of the stone blocks on which the rails and spreader bars (primitive sleepers) were mounted still visible. As you approach the road, you pass some ruins to the left of the track. These are the remains of Garnddyrys Row, part of a village that, in 1851, had a population of some 300 people. More ruins and rubble lie strewn across the hillside, behind and beyond. Once at the road, cross to the far side and turn left up the hill, go past the crash barriers to a meagre lay-by, then follow a faint path to the left of the obvious wooden electricity poles, soon passing a low, orange 'Iron Mountain Trail' waymark and entering an area of overgrown foundations and walls. You are now on the site of Garnddyrys Forge.

Built in 1817, Garnddyrys Forge was where the pig iron from the Blaenavon furnaces (transported along Hill's Tramroad via the Pwll Du tunnel) was converted into more malleable wrought iron – a highly skilled and extremely strenuous process. The workers would have lived in Garnddyrys village. At its height, the forge produced about 200 tons of iron per week, and it remained an important site until production was moved to the new Forgeside Works in Blaenavon, in the early 1860s. An unlikely spot for a foundry, being on an open mountainside at an elevation of 400 metres, it is an atmospheric place where you can easily spend a half-hour exploring.

At the second 'Iron Mountain Trail' waymark, a rough track descends from the road above and curves down towards the valley, while directly in front is the flat and often boggy site of the lower reservoir. Walk down to the right edge of the reservoir and follow the remains of the retaining bank towards the obvious continuation of Hill's Tramroad, clinging to the steep left slopes of the valley ahead. At the far end of the reservoir, look back to the right to see several large blocks of solid iron slag – surreal, iconic sculptures up to 5 metres in height – then continue on any of several routes to gain the obvious shelf on the left side of the valley in front, and follow an impressive section of tramroad as it makes its unlikely way across very steep ground to reach the stream at the head of the valley. The original bridge is long gone, but unless the weather has been particularly inclement, it is seldom a problem to ford the stream and continue on the far side, shortly reaching a junction with an inclined track – Rhiw Ifor – where there is a finger post.

To return directly to the car park, turn left up this track to reach the main road (where there is another finger post), then turn right to reach the entrance to the car park. This results in a walk of just over 5 kilometres. You can also walk directly to this point from the car park, thus shortening the complete walk by a similar distance.

Continue straight ahead at the same level, soon reaching another waymark where the tramroad curves to the left. Do not go any further along the tramroad, but follow the direction indicated by the waymark,

*The surreal sculptures of solid iron slag – the iconic view of Garnddyrys.*

climbing up and to the left along a ridge of spoil where there are good views over Pwll Du Quarry to the right, the masonry of the shaft that housed the water balance hoist in the foreground, and the cutting taken by the continuation of Hill's Tramroad at the far end of the main quarry face. Continue on a narrow path across the steep ground, and then follow any of several indistinct paths through clumps of bilberry, soon climbing a steep bank to reach the (now drained) reservoir that once supplied water to the balance hoist. Turn right along the top of the bank, follow the path around the end of the reservoir, then continue across a very boggy area on strategically placed slabs of rock (some of which may be slightly submerged after wet weather!). The path is fairly obvious on the far side, passing to the left of a wall to reach a kissing gate. Follow the continuation path straight on past a caravan to reach yet another kissing gate, beyond which you follow a track up and to the left, past The Lamb and Fox pub, to reach a road.

You are now standing by all that is left of the village of Pwll Du, once a bustling village housing the families of over 300 miners, iron workers, quarrymen and tramroad workers. In addition to several terraces of houses,

*ABOVE* Hill's Tramroad beyond Garnddyrys.

*RIGHT* Hill's Tramroad between Garnddyrys and Pwll Du – a staggering feat of Victorian engineering – a level shelf cut across the steep hillside.

there was a school, a shop, two pubs, two chapels, and several bakeries. As the local iron and coal industries went into decline, so did the village. In 1960, Pwll Du village was declared a slum, and in 1963 most of the remaining residents were relocated to nearby Govilon. All the buildings were then demolished, save two – one of the pubs (now The Lamb and Fox), and the welfare hall (now an Outdoor Education Centre).

If you wish to visit the Pwll Du Tunnel, turn right and follow the road until you are opposite the Outdoor Education Centre. The bricked-up entrance is in a shallow cutting to the right of the road. For most of its life, horse-drawn tramcars travelled through the tunnel on a single track; and during its busiest periods, trains of between 15 and 20 trams, each carrying about 2 tons of limestone, would pass through the tunnel from Pwll Du to Blaenavon, the trams travelling in the opposite direction carrying pig iron destined for Garnddyrys Forge. Bell wires were used to control movements within the tunnel. Coal was also mined from the

side of the main tunnel, and it is said that when the women of Pwll Du wished to visit the bright lights of Blaenavon, they would ride through the tunnel seated on the trams.

Almost directly opposite The Lamb and Fox, your

*Pwll Du Quarry, with Gilwern Hill in the background. Hill's Tramroad once traversed the top section of the quarry, starting from the fence near the bottom left of the picture, and exiting into a cutting behind the cliff face above left centre. The remains of the water-balance pit are visible as a dark hole, slightly below and right of centre.*

The now drained reservoir that used to feed the
Pwll Du Quarry water-balance hoist.

onward route lies up the wide, rocky track that heads straight up the hill-side. This is the line of a double incline built in 1850 by Thomas Dyne-Steel, Assistant Manager and Engineer of the Blaenavon Ironworks. Powered initially by steam, and later by electricity, this was an effective and efficient way of moving pig iron and raw materials over the mountain, and it soon replaced the Pwll Du tunnel as the main transport route. Despite this, records show that limestone was still being carried through the tunnel from the Pwll Du and Tyla quarries as late as 1926, the horses having by this time been replaced by stationary engines at either end of the tunnel.

Towards the top of the hill, bear left, heading towards the distant remains of a brick-built generator building, the track and the surroundings increasingly black with coal – the remains of past opencast activity. A short distance further, bear to the right and continue climbing past some concrete posts, soon passing to the left of the old generator house. Bear slightly left along an obvious track, then continue straight ahead through a shallow cutting to follow the Dyne-Steel Incline, straight

*One of the entrances to the Pwll Du Tunnel as it is today.*
*The grille is there to allow bats to pass freely.*

*The Dyne-Steel incline – a linear scar across an already ravaged landscape. Despite its almost surgically precise straight course and modern efficiency, the Pwll Du Tunnel (which it was supposed to replace) continued to carry limestone until well into the twentieth century.*

as an arrow down the bleak hillside. The track gets progressively muddier as you descend, but nowhere is it so bad that you cannot progress with reasonably dry feet – although you may have to choose your route with care.

At the far side of the small reservoir (on the left towards the bottom), turn left on to a better track, and head towards the distant but obvious stone pillar of the Hill Pits Chimney, the walking now much easier (apart from one stream, currently and possibly temporarily crossed by a strange plank bridge). As you wander, muse upon the fact that, prior to the Industrial Revolution, this whole area was bleak moorland, sparsely populated by subsistence farmers. There were few settlements, and those that did exist were small and isolated. As happened at Merthyr Tydfil, the coming of iron and coal changed everything, for within less than a decade the local population had exploded as literally thousands of people travelled to the area in search of a better life – something easier than living off the land. For the vast majority, what they found was neither easier nor better. Housing conditions ranged from basic to appalling, sanitation

*The Big Pit Mining Museum, seen from the Dyne-Steel incline, is a significant part of the landscape, beyond an old supply reservoir. Capturing both the spirit and reality of a Welsh coal mine, this is a deservedly popular tourist attraction, and worthy of a visit when the hills are cloaked with clag.*

was virtually non-existent, disease was rife, and working conditions were harsh to the extreme. Life was cheap, and injuries and deaths were an almost daily occurrence.

But it was not all negative! The shared hardships created strong community bonds, and this, in turn, lead to a cultural explosion epitomised by the likes of eisteddfodau and male voice choirs. While there were undoubtedly terrible acts of exploitation, there were also great acts of philanthropy. Not only were museums, schools and hospitals built, but also several charitable institutions were founded. Trades unions and political parties were formed, Chartists and Suffragettes protested what they believed to be just causes and communities were born and nurtured.

Hill Pits mine dates from the 1830s, and was dug in order to supply both coal and iron ore to the Blaenavon Ironworks. The chimney is all that remains of the pit's steam-driven winding engine, and although it is a local landmark, how long it will remain standing is uncertain for, as you will see, its face is split by a long, vertical crack – possibly a result of the

*Hill Pits Chimney – a crumbling monument to a bygone time. Big Pit is obvious to the right, while the onward route follows the base of the spoil heap to the left.*

tree that has taken root on top. Follow the track until you are just past the chimney, then turn right on to another track and start to descend, the rusting ends of several tramroad rails just visible above the rocky surface. Pass a small grove of hawthorns on the left (probably the remains of an old hedge, judging by their shape), and just before the main track curves right, turn left on to a much grassier path that curves around the front of the spoil to your left, running parallel to a line of wooden electricity poles. You soon pass under the electricity cables and the path curves to the right and starts to descend, soon reaching a gate. Go through this, and continue through more gates to reach a surfaced lane where you bear right to reach the main road. Cross to the pavement and turn left, then continue straight on for just over 300 metres, past two turnings on the right (the first has a sign welcoming you to Blaenavon), until – at the end of a clump of trees – three large wooden posts mark the start of a narrow and sometimes overgrown fenced path that leads down the left side of the wood to a stile, beyond which the path more-or-less follows the line of the fence to yet another stile. Cross this and turn left alongside the fence, soon reaching a corridor between two playing fields, at the far end of which a better track continues straight ahead. Blaenavon Ironworks are hidden behind the fence and vegetation to the right, and you soon get a good view of part of the site through a large access gate at the far end of the track. Walk straight on through the yard of a car repair workshop to reach a lane. Although your onward route is to the left, it is definitely worth visiting the Blaenavon Ironworks, only a short distance away. To do this, turn right, follow the lane down to the main road, and then turn right again.

Blaenavon Ironworks, founded in 1789, is one of the most important sites to have survived from the early years of the Industrial Revolution. At its height, there were six blast furnaces in operation here, all built into the hillside in such a way that raw materials could be tipped in from above. In the 1870s, two cousins – Percy Gilchrist and Sidney Gilchrist-Thomas – perfected a way of producing better quality mild steel, which involved using special perforated round bricks called 'Bessemer Tuyeres'. Within ten years, ironworks all over the world were investing in the new process. This fascinating site contains not only the remains of the blast furnaces, but also the workers' housing, and is currently under the care of Cadw, the official guardian of Welsh built heritage. Visitor facilities include excellent interpretive information boards and exhibitions, an information centre and shop staffed by friendly people, and toilets. Admission is free, and the site is definitely worth a visit. The area known as Stack Square was the setting of an excellent BBC Wales reality series *Coal House*.

Having explored, retrace your steps to the lane beyond the car repair workshop, and continue up the hill to reach a main road. Cross this

*Stack Square, Blaenavon Ironworks – so named because of the remains of an old chimney in its midst. This was the setting for an excellent BBC Wales reality programme –* Coal House *– which explored the issues facing families living in a mining community in the early years of the twentieth century.*

and follow the obvious path on the far side, curving up and around to reach the Rifle Green car park, on the site of Bunkers Row, where there were originally two terraces of ironworkers' housing. Turn left in front of the information board, and keep left along a grassy path through a belt of trees, eventually merging with a better, rutted track where you should turn right. The wall on the left is built almost entirely of Bessemer Tuyeres – the round bricks that revolutionised the steel-making process – and the nearby ruins mark the site of the Upper Brickyard, where the bricks that lined the furnaces were made. This incredibly heavy work was done predominantly by young women and girls, who trod fireclay into a useable consistency and then moulded it into bricks, which were then dried before being fired in kilns. Such was the demand for these bricks that they were often unloaded from the kilns while they were still hot, so burns and heat injuries were common.

Keep left up the track, following the line of wooden electricity poles and walking parallel to the road, soon reaching the entrance drive of the Wyndee Kennels. Cross the main road to the right, then turn left along the grass verge, past a playing field, to reach a cattle grid. A short distance further on, bear right past a vehicle barrier to gain a rough track, and follow this for some distance through old spoil heaps. Take the left-hand fork near the top, and then continue to a finger post where you turn left on to a faint path leading to a tiny valley where, in wet weather, you will share the path with a stream (easily avoided on the right). This valley is not natural, but was formed by early miners in their search for minerals. Where minerals were close to the surface, they were exposed by 'scouring', a process in which streams and springs were dammed to form small pools, which were then allowed to escape in torrents which washed away the topsoil.

Continue along the now more obvious path as it exits the left side of the valley and wends its way through the heather, passing a waymark and a couple of sandy pools, to reach a lane, glancing behind for views of the distant Bristol Channel. Turn left along the lane to reach the road, and then turn right to return to the Keepers Pond car park.

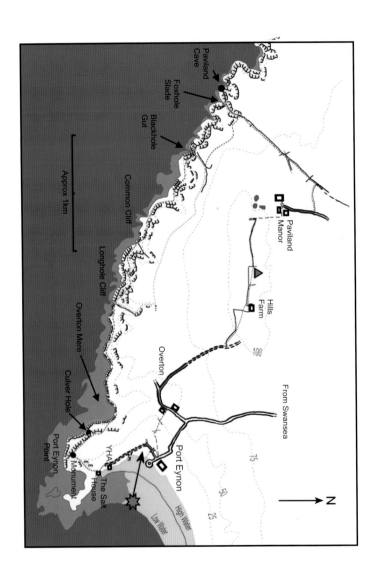

Paviland Cave

Foxhole Slade

Blackhole Gut

Approx 1km

Common Cliff

Longhole Cliff

Overton Mere

Culver Hole

Port Eynon Point

Paviland Manor

Hills Farm

Overton

From Swansea

Port Eynon

YHA

Monument

The Salt House

High Water

Low Water

100

75

50

25

15

N

# 7.
# SALT, SMUGGLERS & RED LADIES

An exploratory ramble along a magnificent coastline frequented by smugglers, cave bears, pigeon farmers and salt collectors. The outward route includes some of the finest cliff walking in Britain, while the return journey provides a contrast, crossing ancient meadows and farmland.

## BACKGROUND INFORMATION

**Location** The south-western coastline of the Gower Peninsula, the first place in Britain to be designated as an Area of Outstanding Natural Beauty.

**Start & finish point** Port Eynon car park (SS468851 – pay & display).

**Maps needed** OS Explorer 164.

**Map distance** 12 kilometres.

**Height gain** 300 metres.

**Terrain** Reasonable coastal paths, with some rocky sections and large drops. The path occasionally forces its way through clumps of gorse, so shorts are not recommended. Like much coastal walking, the route constantly varies from uphill to downhill, making it surprisingly tiring and difficult to judge distances. The return journey is across farmland on tracks and paths, some of which can be muddy and heavily overgrown.

**Duration** Allow 4 hours plus exploration time.

**Hazards** Cliff edges. Some of the cliff paths are narrow and rocky, and traverse steep cliffs, sometimes very close to significant drops, although there is an easier alternative. The optional detours to Culver Hole and Paviland Cave should only be attempted one hour either side of low tide.

**Public transport** Port Eynon has only an infrequent bus service, particularly during winter months. The nearest railway station is at Swansea.

**Amenities/facilities** Port Eynon virtually shuts down during the winter months, but is a busy place in the summer when the gift shops and tourist cafes do a roaring trade. There is a village shop, a youth hostel, and several guest houses, and there are public toilets by the car park. More facilities (post office, etc.) are available near by at Scurlage and Reynoldston, and the bright lights of Swansea are only a short distance further.

COASTAL WALKING IS SUCH A TACTILE EXPERIENCE! Not only is there the sound, sight and smell of the sea, there is also the tang of salt on your lips, and the sea breezes that play with your hair. And when the coast is that of the Gower Peninsula, with some of the most magnificent coastal scenery in Britain, and a landscape heritage that stretches back over 26,000 years, the walking cannot fail to impress.

This is indisputably one of my favourite coastal areas, and I have spent countless hours here, walking (and climbing) the cliffs; exploring the caves and rock pools; and seeking out the less well-known nooks and crannies. There is so much of interest in such a compact area that I found it very difficult to choose which walk to include in this book. It is well nigh impossible to do justice to the area during a single visit, but hopefully my final choice of route will give you a flavour of this most captivating coastline.

The walk starts from Port Eynon, a village near the most southerly point on Gower. Eynon was an eleventh-century Welsh prince who supposedly built a cliff-top castle here, although there is nothing to show where it stood. Lobsters, crabs and oysters have all provided a living for local people over the years, and the remains of oyster pools and an old harbour wall are still visible at low tide. Smuggling was a popular pastime in the area throughout the seventeenth, eighteenth and nineteenth centuries, and records show that as many as eight excise men were once stationed here. Now a popular spot with water sports enthusiasts and holiday makers, you will need to get to the car park early during sunny summer weekends if you wish to find a space.

Your first objective is the Youth Hostel, the obvious building close to the shore on the way to the point. At low tide, you can approach this by walking along the beach at the right side of the bay. If the water is high, however, it is better to follow the rough lane that runs alongside the most southerly of the two parking areas, heading towards Port Eynon Point past Port Eynon Boat Club car park. Ignoring the concrete slipway leading to the beach, continue straight ahead to reach the youth hostel.

Despite its popularity with sailors and surfers, the coastline around here is notorious for ship wrecks, and the treacherous rocks and sandbanks are unforgiving to any vessel that strays too close. In 1884, Port Eynon Bay was the site of a tragedy when the *Agnes Jack* steamship

*The Salt House, looking towards Port Eynon. Note the modern sea wall to the right, protecting what is left of the structure.*

was driven on to the rocks in a storm, and the villagers could do nothing but watch helplessly as the entire crew of twenty-five men were drowned. As a result, a lifeboat station was established here, and the lifeboat served the south Gower coast for many years. In 1916, however, tragedy struck again, and three lifeboat crew were killed while going to the assistance of the Glasgow steamship *Dunvegan*. A memorial to the men was erected in the local church, and by 1919, the lifeboat station had been closed, the decision having been made that it was the in wrong location for so dangerous an area. A new inshore lifeboat station was eventually opened in 1968 at Horton, at the opposite end of the beach, and the original lifeboat station building now houses the youth hostel.

Continue along the beach (at low tide) or the lane (at high tide – passing through a caravan site that appears to be a haven for thousands of rabbits), soon reaching substantial ruins at the far end of the bay. These are the remains of a Salt House. The sea water along this stretch of coast has a particularly high salinity, which makes it ideal as a source of sea salt. The sea water was partly evaporated in shallow chambers, then boiled

*View west from the headland above Port Eynon Point.*

in large lead or iron pans in order to crystallise the salt, which was then used for curing meat or fish. The first salt house is believed to have been built in the reign of Henry VIII by David Lucas, and it is said that his son, John, later fortified it and used it as a base for piracy and smuggling. Although there is no direct evidence of this, smuggling appears to have been endemic in the area from as early as the sixteenth century, so the story may not be totally apocryphal. The building was largely destroyed by a great storm in the early 1700s, the current remains being protected from further damage by a concrete sea wall. There is a good information board on site.

The whole of the Gower Peninsula has a fascinating geomorphology, and nowhere more so than around Port Eynon Point, just beyond the Salt House. Those of you interested in such things will find wave cut platforms and raised beaches, while others more interested in the marine environment will find plenty of superb rock pools. Additionally, Gower is renowned for being one of the richest archaeological areas in Wales, and many important remains have been unearthed from the numerous sea caves that riddle the coastline hereabouts. The nearby Port Eynon Point

*The enigmatic Culver Hole – a simple pigeon house, or something more?*

Cave, for example, contained several remains including the bones of red deer, bear, lion, woolly rhinoceros, and mammoth. If you decide to explore near the shoreline, please remember that the tide comes in with surprising speed along this section of the coast, and it is frighteningly easy to get cut off owing to the complex nature of the terrain, and difficult to escape from the incoming tide owing to the steepness of the cliffs.

From the Salt House, make your way up on to the headland, heading for the obvious obelisk along a narrow and sometime steep, loose and rocky path that meanders through ancient quarries. The views open out as you reach the top, but beware the very steep drops immediately beyond the obelisk – a memorial to the founders of the Gower Society. Follow the now grassy path along the top of the headland with the coast to your left, the mournful tolling of a nearby bell-buoy, very obvious (particularly when there is an onshore breeze). After only a short distance, you descend steeply into Overton Mere, a very rocky, circular bay.

Although your onward route continues around the bay, it is well worth making the effort to reach Culver Hole, an enigmatic ruin that lies hidden near by. Please note, however, that you should only follow this detour if the tide is low and still on its way out. To reach the ruin, make your way carefully down on to the rocks, then turn left and scramble awkwardly around the headland, glancing back and to the left until you see a narrow cleft with masonry at its far end. This is Culver Hole, about which there are

*View west across Overton Mere from above Culver Hole.*

many stories, most of them associated with smuggling, and some sources suggest that John Lucas hid his contraband and weapons here. The ruin has also been linked with the Salt House and with the elusive Port Eynon Castle and, perhaps unsurprisingly, there are several references to secret passageways! Entry can be gained by climbing the rope that hangs from the door, but this is a precarious undertaking and more than a few will choose to examine the site from no closer than the relative safety of the beach! Beyond the door is a large platform from where a stone staircase leads up to four further floors. There are also numerous nesting holes, which gives a clue to the true use of the site, for Culver Hole is now believed to have been a pigeon house, built to provide a source of eggs and fresh meat! Indeed, 'Culfre' is an old English word meaning pigeon, and there are similar pigeon houses at nearby Oxwich and Penrice castles. By all means take your time exploring, but do not get caught by the tide – the terrain is surprisingly awkward with many rock pools blocking a direct route back to the path, and it is easy to underestimate how long the return trip will take.

*Heading towards Longhole. The white dot in the distance
is a person standing beside the ruined limekiln!*

Back at Overton Mere, follow the coast path as it curves around the back of the main bay. Come here at the right time of year, and you will be surrounded by a profusion of wild flowers. Keep close to the sea, ignoring any paths that veer inland, and continue around the next (smaller) bay towards Overton Cliff, the views back towards Port Eynon Point getting better with each step. The path, however, starts to get a little rougher, and you need to take care as there are some significant drops to the left, very close to the path . . . mere precursors for what is to come! At the end of the bay, the path climbs slightly to negotiate the headland, then continues below a large cliff with an obvious cave entrance some distance above the ground, soon reaching a large but narrow valley with a rocky gorge at its inland end. A sign here informs you that you are at Longhole Cliff, one of several nature reserves along the South Gower coastline.

Longhole Cliff is named after a nearby cave which was excavated by archaeologists in the nineteenth century, and which yielded Stone Age tools and a variety of remains of Ice Age animals (now on display in Swansea Museum). The ruin just beyond the fence is that of a limekiln, which burned the limestone from the nearby quarries, the resulting lime being spread on the local fields to try and offset the acidity caused, in part, by the salt air. The nature reserve clearly displays the differences between vegetation growing in the deeper cliff-top soils (such as gorse) and the thinner soils found on the cliffs and scree (such as limestone grasses and flowers).

If you wish to avoid the steeper cliffs and bigger drops, it is now that you should head inland, following the path through the valley, and then climbing to reach a good cliff-top path. Turn left and follow this along the tops of the cliffs for just over 2 kilometres, mostly alongside walls and fences, to reach Foxhole Slade – a narrow, gorge like valley with a stone wall running down the middle. The views are stunning throughout.

To continue along the main route, walk past the ruined limekiln, climb the path on to the headland, then follow the path that traverses the slopes beyond. This is coastal walking at its best – each headland bringing a new horizon, each horizon more breathtaking than the last. Your eyes will undoubtedly be drawn to the views, but if you wish to admire them, make sure you stop, for the path is tricky and extremely airy in parts, and some of the drops are considerable. This is not the place for those with no head for heights! Past the biggest drop so far, the path eases somewhat and descends slightly, only to climb again towards an obvious U-shaped groove between a very steep cliff on the right and an ivy covered buttress on the left. The views open out once again as you walk through the groove, and you may find yourself in company, as the cliff to the right is beloved of rock climbers.

Beyond the groove, a narrow valley heads inland, the path still obvious on the far side. Descend into the valley and then follow the path on to the next headland; the roar of surf a constant in your left ear, the music of birdsong in your right. If you are wearing shorts, you may dislike this section, for there is a fair amount of gorse. Eventually you reach a stone wall, which you should cross at its extreme left end, then follow the path that climbs steeply on to the next headland. At the top of this, keep left, and start heading downhill, following an unlikely looking route that appears, at first, to be leading you towards the top of a steep cliff. Very soon, however, a grassy terrace appears. Carefully zigzag down on to this terrace in order to gain a grassy path, and then follow this past some strange

*Looking towards Common Cliff from the top of the U-shaped groove beyond Longhole Cliff. Worm's Head is obvious on the horizon.*

*The strange rock sculptures on the descent at Common Cliff.*

*The airy path leading from Common Cliff towards Blackhole Gut, with incomparable coastal scenery.*

rock sculptures on the left, descending into another large valley at Common Cliff.

Once again, cross the valley and continue along the coastal path, eventually climbing steeply on to yet another headland, this time making for an obvious groove, just above the steepest part of the cliff to the left. At the top, an extremely airy path follows a narrow rock ledge across the cliff beyond. Most people will find the initial move on to the ledge fairly exciting, and even though the terrain eases as you progress across the face, this section will almost certainly raise adrenalin levels. Indeed, non-climbers may find the whole of this section intimidating. And it does not end there, for only a short distance beyond, the path curves to the right and reaches the head of Blackhole Gut, a vertical-sided zawn that slices into the landscape. This is a very exposed spot, and is particularly atmospheric if there is a high tide and a large swell, for you can feel the ground tremble as the waves pound the inner reaches of the zawn.

The cliffs beyond Blackhole Gut become increasingly steep and complex, and while it is possible to continue all the way to the coastal end of Foxhole Slade, this is not to be recommended – certainly not in a book of

*Blackhole Gut from the path – not a good place if you suffer from vertigo!*

this type! So it is here that you must make your way up on to the top of the cliff. From the head of Blackhole Gut, do not follow the path around to the left, but continue directly ahead, climbing steeply and carefully up grassy, boulder-strewn slopes, heading for either of two small but obvious U-shaped notches on the skyline. At the top, the angle eases and you find yourself on pleasant, level ground at the top of the cliffs. Bear to the right, and then walk directly away from the cliff edge with your back to the sea, aiming to reach the well-trodden cliff-top path. If you come to a wire fence, turn right and follow this to reach the path at a gate; if you come to an old earth wall, turn left and follow the path to the same gate.

Go through the kissing gate, take the left branch of the path beyond, and enter a different world. The roar of the surf diminishes to a background suggestion, and the mewling of seabirds is replaced by a surround-sound of meadow song and grasshoppers, the sea breezes whispering through the long grass. Walking suddenly becomes delightfully easy, for instead of rocks and drops you tread a wide, level path of soft, sheep-cropped turf.

*Foxhole Slade. Paviland Cave can be reached at low tide by scrambling across the seaward face of the steep headland to the right.*

Continue blissfully until you reach a sudden hiatus – a deep, narrow, steep sided valley cutting across the landscape. This is Foxhole Slade, easily identifiable by the stone wall that runs along its base. Carefully follow the path into the base of the valley to reach a stile where there is a sign informing you that you are about to enter the South Gower Nature Reserves. Do not cross this stile!

It is here that the easier cliff top detour and the more adventurous main route merge.

Although your onward path lies along the path to your right, you might like to make a short but steep detour down through the valley to your left, following a reasonable if sometimes overgrown path along the nearside of the wall, reaching the very rocky shoreline at the bottom – an atmospheric place. A short distance away, across the rocks on the far side of the inlet, lies Paviland Cave, one of the most famous archaeological caves in the world. The large, pear-shaped entrance is just above the waterline, and is only accessible at low tide. The chamber within is illuminated by daylight issuing from a hole in the roof, over 20 metres above. Please note that the cave is only accessible at low tide, and is dangerous at all other times, and be warned that escape is extremely difficult if you get caught by the rising tide in this area.

Paviland Cave, the earliest scientifically excavated cave in the British Isles, is home to the oldest known human burial in Britain, and the oldest known ceremonial burial in Western Europe. It was during excavations done by the Reverend William Buckley in 1823 that an adult human skeleton was found. Guided by his devout religious beliefs, the Reverend Buckley fervently believed that no human remains had survived the Great Flood, so he reasoned that the remains must be Roman. Because of the decorative items buried with the body – items made from bone, antler and ivory, together with seashell necklaces – Buckley reasoned that the body was that of a woman. Furthermore, the bones were red in colour owing to the ochre that had been sprinkled over the body at the time of death. Taking all the evidence into account, the Reverend concluded that the body was that of a Roman prostitute or possibly a witch, and he named her 'The Red Lady of Paviland'. Unfortunately, all his conclusions were wrong. Modern tests have shown that the body is that of a young man, possibly in his early twenties, and dates from the Upper Palaeolithic period, making him some 26,000 years old!

In addition to the famous body, many other important remains and artefacts have been found here, including over 4,000 worked flints, necklace bones, stone needles and ivory bracelets (the ivory originating from mammoths), and Paviland is internationally recognised as an exceptionally valuable archaeological site. Given the nature of his burial, it is now believed that the young man must have been an important person, and that the cave was a significant Shamanic site.

Retrace your steps up through the valley, passing a large rock shelter below an overhanging cliff (on the left near the top). Twenty-six thousand years ago, this would have been a valuable piece of real estate, and people would almost certainly have lived here. At the junction with the coast path, do not cross the wall to the left, but continue to follow it inland, almost immediately reaching a ladder stile with a yellow waymark. Cross the stile, and follow the obvious path to the right of an overgrown field boundary, climbing slightly, to reach another stile. Cross this and continue in the same direction, climbing gently alongside farmland, still with the overgrown field boundary to the left, eventually crossing two more stiles with a footbridge in between. Keep heading in the same direction with a hedge to your left (another hedge veers off to the right towards farm

*Looking towards Port Eynon point from near the ruined Hills farm.*
*The faint path heads almost straight towards the headland.*

buildings at this point) and follow the edge of the field until you reach a ditch crossed by a wooden footbridge with a handrail. Do not cross this bridge, but turn right and follow a faint path alongside the ditch to reach the far side of the field, where there is a further stile leading to a lane. The path across the field, although reasonably obvious, gets heavily overgrown, and you need to take care not to stray on to the field or, worse, fall into the ditch!

Once across the stile, turn right down the lane towards Paviland Manor. On reaching the buildings, turn left immediately beyond the first barn (waymarked), walk between the two buildings, then continue to the end of the concrete hardstanding to reach a farm track on the right, which climbs gently up the right side of a field. Although waymarked, this route is not the same as the right of way indicated on OS maps. Follow the track to the top of the hill, then turn left along an often very overgrown path that runs along the top of the field, with the hedge to your right and wide views towards Worms Head to your left.

At the end of the field is a very overgrown stile. Cross this into much easier terrain – grazed land with many thistles – and walk straight across the field (avoiding the cowpats!) heading for an obvious gate and stile on the far side. Cross this stile and continue across the next field with a trig point to your left, heading towards the right-hand side of the derelict Hills Farm. Just before the ruin, there is another gate and overgrown stile on the right. Cross this and immediately turn left, making for another stile straight in front. Once you have crossed this, bear to the right across the field, heading straight towards the distant headland on the far side of Port Eynon Bay, trending right to reach the fence where it bends sharply to the south. Follow this fence down towards the end of the narrowing field, now heading straight towards Port Eynon Point, eventually reaching another overgrown stile. Cross this and bear round to the left, to reach a green lane, where you should turn right. The short section between the stile and the green lane is sometimes heavily overgrown. I find it interesting that, while so much effort has obvious been made to keep the (upper) coast path in a good state of repair, little appears to be done in the way of maintenance to any of the paths further inland.

Follow the sometimes muddy green lane between high hedges, the surface slowly improving as you descend, eventually reaching a surfaced lane where you continue straight on. This lane leads to the charming village of Overton, and where the road forks around a small green, keep to the left, the sound of distant surf starting to become obvious again. Start to climb, then a short distance after a large building on the right, and just before the row of buildings on the left, cross a stile on the right (signposted to Port Eynon) into a field often full of caravans. Go straight across the field to another stile, cross this, then continue in the same direction, passing to the left of a double telegraph pole with a transformer on it, to reach another stile, beyond which is a caravan park. Walk straight through the caravan park, along a lane (with a no entry sign) between rows of permanent caravans, soon reaching a vehicle barrier just before the village road. Turn right through a gap in the wall immediately before the road, and thus return to the car park.

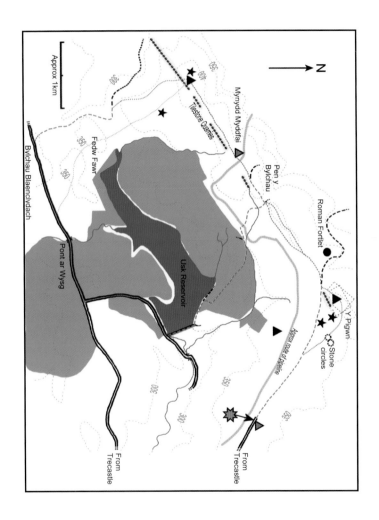

N

Approx 1km

Bwlchau Blaenclydach

Fedw Fawr

Tilestone Quarries

Mynydd Myddfai

Pen y Bwlchau

Pont ar Wysg

Usk Reservoir

Roman Fortlet

Approx route of pipeline

Stone circles

Y Pigwn

300

350

350

300

300

350

400

350

300

From Trecastle

From Trecastle

# 8.
# MARCHING WITH THE
# LEGIONNAIRES

*A panoramic slice through history, taking in a wild common, a majestic ridge, and a drowned valley, all of which have been used and abused from ancient times to the present day.*

## BACKGROUND INFORMATION

**Location** Mynydd Myddfai, between Sennybridge and Llandovery, in the north-west of the Brecon Beacons National Park.

**Start & finish point** Rough parking area at SN845300, at the gate marking the end of the tarmac lane from Trecastle.

**Maps needed** OS Explorer OL12.

**Map distance** 20 kilometres.

**Height gain** 350 metres.

**Terrain** A mixed bag of quiet lanes, forest tracks, good paths, and sheep tracks, with one relatively straightforward cross-country section.

**Duration** Allow 6 hours.

**Hazards** Potentially tricky navigation at the western end of the Mynydd Myddfai ridge, some sections of which can be muddy after inclement weather.

**Public transport** The nearest bus route is at Trecastle, and the nearest railway station is at Llandovery.

**Amenities/facilities** The village of Trecastle has a few rural facilities including a village shop, an excellent bunkhouse and an ancient coaching inn. Somewhat more urban facilities can be found in Llandovery and Brecon.

CALL ME CYNICAL IF YOU WILL, but I sometimes question the worth of conservation legislation. There seems little point in designating any area as worthy of conservation if such designation is ignored whenever it is deemed inconvenient. Take the recent construction of a high pressure gas pipeline between Felindre (near Swansea) and Tirley in Gloucestershire. Not only does this run through a section of the Brecon Beacons National Park that is a designated area of Outstanding Natural Beauty with unique geological characteristics and special UNESCO Geopark status, but it also impacts upon at least one Site of Special

Scientific Interest (SSSI), and affects several ancient remains, some dating from before the Iron Age. As for the assurances that the land would be reinstated to the highest environmental standards . . . what utter poppycock! While it might be feasible to rebuild a ploughed field, I fail to see how it is possible to recreate a large tract of upland common which has remained virtually untouched for 2,000 years. But it doesn't really matter what I think, for you will be able to make up your own mind about such things during this walk.

To be fair, the upland commons of Mynydd Bach Trecastell and Mynydd Myddfai have been used and abused for millennia. In ancient times, Bronze and Iron Age people lived and worked here, leaving behind them a profusion of stone circles and burial cairns. Then the Romans invaded, building roads, encampments and forts, and exploiting the local natural resources, as exemplified at the nearby Dolaucothi gold mines, worked by the Romans from about AD 75. When they left, this Roman legacy was built upon by their successors, from the Normans (who built castle mounds within Roman defensive sites) to the Tudors (who used the original Roman road across the high moors as the basis for the coach road between Brecon and Llandovery). More recently, in the eighteenth and nineteenth centuries, local folk scratched a meagre living from the land by quarrying tilestones from the high ridge, and then in the twentieth century, the valley to the south was flooded in order to provide a water supply for Swansea. So much history in such a small area.

The best approach to the start of the walk is from the village of Trecastle, which lies on the A40 between Brecon and Llandovery. At the western edge of the village, take a narrow street heading south-west (to the left when facing Llandovery), soon leaving the houses behind and climbing steeply. Just before the top of the hill, turn suddenly right on to an even narrower but predominantly straight lane – the line of the Roman road – and continue for some distance with increasing numbers of potholes. The views across to the Carmarthen Fan, to the left, soon become truly spectacular, while the views to the right are pretty good as well. You also get a great panorama of the central Brecon Beacons in your rear view mirror! Eventually, you reach a gate at the end of the tarmac, where there is sufficient room for two or three cars to park. Don't worry

*Usk Reservoir from the Roman road, the once open common now hideously marred by a succession of fences, guarding the gas pipeline.*

if you hear the sound of artillery and gunfire – the huge Sennybridge Training Area (SENTA in army speak) is only a short distance to the north, and it often makes its presence felt most audibly.

Go through the gate and follow the now rough track across Mynydd Bach Trecastell, heading directly towards a low rounded dome on the horizon. This hill is called Y Pigwn (literally, The Cone) and is the site of two Roman marching camps. The disturbed ground running alongside you to your left (and, later, to your right) is possibly the original line of the Roman road (or perhaps an even earlier route), while the present track is the somewhat more modern line of the medieval coach road. The Usk Reservoir soon appears from behind a slight rise to the left, the once-open views across the common now marred by a succession of fenced corridors highlighting the already obvious line of the gas pipeline. I have no idea how permanent these fences will be, but judging by other similar works in the area, it is likely that they will remain in place for many years, a hideous linear blot across the landscape.

The Roman road across Mynydd Bach Trecastle, with the low dome of Y Pigwn forming the horizon. The embankment of one of the marching camps is just discernable as a horizontal line, with a right-angled corned at its right end.

A fence and old wall soon come close to the right side of the track, and as you gain the first rise, you may be able to see a long, straight line running across the face of Y Pigwn, with a noticeable right-angled bend at its right-hand end. This line marks the embankment of one of the rectangular Roman marching camps, more of which anon. The fence to the right soon turns away from the track, and you continue along the line of the Roman road, later used by the coach road between Brecon and Llandovery. Although you can continue along the track to reach the left side of Y Pigwn directly, by detouring along a faint but obvious path that bears off to the right, just beyond the next rise, you will soon reach Cerrig y Pigwn, where there are two stone circles dating from the late Neolithic or early Bronze Age (which makes them about 4,000 years old). The main circle is just under 25 metres in diameter and consists of 28 small stones. The smaller circle is just over 7 metres in diameter and consists of only four large stones, although there are several holes near by, which suggests that some stones are missing.

*Mynydd Myddfai from the Roman road. The walk follows the skyline from right to left.*

Whichever route you choose, you should eventually make your way up on to the top of Y Pigwn, the obvious highpoint ahead, where there are good panoramic views. You are now standing in the middle of two large, rectangular Roman marching camps, one slightly smaller than the other, the smaller one superimposed upon (and thus post-dating) the larger. The camps are believed to have been constructed, a few years apart, by Roman legionaries and auxiliaries during two separate summer campaigns in the early AD 70s. Both comprise an area enclosed by earth and turf banks, inside which the soldiers pitched their heavy leather tents. The banks would originally have been surmounted by a palisade of wooden stakes, with a defensive ditch in front.

The Roman armies probably used these camps as their main base as they struck out into territory occupied by two local Celtic tribes – the Silures to the south-east, and the Demetae to the south-west – and each may have accommodated as many as 10,000 men. These troops would have been under the command of Julius Agricola, Emperor Claudius's son-in-law, who had been given the unenviable task of conquering both Wales and Scotland.

Although their orientation is slightly different, both camps share a common centre point, marked by a low mound – possibly the remains of an assembly area where the main streets converged and altars to the Roman gods were situated. The palisades are long gone, but the central mound and the low, rounded ramparts and external ditches are still just visible (except in the south-eastern corner, where the remains have been destroyed by more recent tilestone quarrying), as are several of the entrances. These all feature curving ramparts called 'claviculae', positioned just inside the entrance gaps, designed to turn attackers' shield arms away from the defenders.

This whole area must have been of strategic and economic importance throughout the Roman occupation, being crossed by the Roman road between Brecon Gaer (an important Roman fort) and Moridunum (Carmarthen), with links to the Roman gold mines at Dolaucothi. Indeed, there are several smaller military sites near by (some of which were later

*Carreg y Pigwn stone circle, looking towards Mynydd Epynt and the Sennybridge Training Area.*

exploited as medieval defences), as well as another huge marching camp to the south at Arhosfa'r Garreg-lwyd, which you will approach later.

Having explored Y Pigwn, make your way back to the Roman road to the south-west, heading directly towards the high ground of Mynydd Myddfai and your onward route – the obvious path along the top of the ridge. On reaching the Roman road, turn right (west), very soon to reach a junction. Straight ahead, after about 400 metres, are the scant and virtually invisible remains of a Roman fortlet on the left, later used as the site for a Norman motte and bailey, also difficult to see. Your route, however, lies to the left, along a less well-defined but rutted and sometimes muddy track leading up on to the high ground, soon cresting the low ridge. The ruts are recent, having been caused by the vehicles used by the pipeline contractors. You are now approaching the start of Mynydd Myddfai – a stunningly panoramic ridge, which you follow for just under 4 kilometres. To the right, beyond Llandovery and the Towy Valley, the fields of Carmarthenshire and the Cambrian Mountains stretch as far as the eye can see; while to the left – beyond the scars of the pipeline, the

*The Usk Reservoir and the distant Carmarthen Fan from the Roman road.*

scientifically important raised bog of Waun Ddu and the Usk Reservoir – the horizon is dominated by the majestic peaks of Y Mynydd Du. Confusingly, this translates to the Black Mountain, leading many people to get confused between the Black Mountain (singular – to the west) and the Black Mountains (plural – to the east). To avoid this confusion, many local people refer to the Black Mountain as the Carmarthen Fan, something I have done in this book.

Ignore tracks to the left and right, and stick to the high ground to get the best views, leaving the most obvious path if necessary. No photograph can do justice to the panorama, nor to the atmosphere of the ridge – you have to experience the pleasure for yourself. And it is not just about the view … keep your eyes open for ravens playing with the wind, for buzzards and red kites soaring on the updraughts; and listen for the delightful music of the skylarks. Additionally, drag your eyes away from the views every now and then to look at your more immediate surroundings, for the land around you is peppered with Bronze Age burial cairns and other ancient remains such as enclosures and standing stones, all dating from between about 1800 and 1200 BC. Once you get beyond the obvious saddle of Pen y Bylchau, where the track surface has, once again, been deeply rutted by

*The Carmarthen Fan from the start of the Mynydd Myddfai ridge.*

the pipeline contractors' vehicles, the slopes to the left are very obviously scarred by what looks like an ancient ditch and rampart system. In fact, these scratches are of more recent origin, believed to be strip quarries dating from the eighteenth century. The objective of these excavations were tilestones – a type of sandstone which cleaves easily into slabs, much valued for flagstones, roofing slabs and general building work. Many of the tracks along the ridge probably owe their existence to these quarries, although it is probable that much earlier ridge top paths existed.

Continue along the top of the ridge, forsaking the obvious track when it heads off to the right. The walking along this section, on or off the track, is delightful – but be prepared for a nasty shock, for as you near the summit of Mynydd Myddfai, you reach another fenced corridor marking the line of the abominable pipeline, which cuts across the summit at 90° to the line of the ridge before veering to the left and dropping into the valley. Cross the dreaded corridor via the two obvious stiles to reach the summit and a trig point.

At the time of writing (early 2009), this whole area seems to be in a state of flux as a direct result of the pipeline. Everywhere you look there are reminders that the supposedly protected common has been abused – the hideous scar of the pipeline with its tangle of fences; ancient trackways churned by four-wheel drive vehicles; battered, white metal discs looking like old dustbin lids, crudely painted with black arrows to show the contractors how to get safely off the hill; mindlessly discarded plastic drinks bottles and worse. A few of these wounds may be healed; several more will fade with time; but a significant number will remain for decades, an unpleasant reminder of a misguided political expedient.

North-west from the trig point, nestling in the valley below, lies the Llwynywormwood Estate, site of one of the 'Lost Houses of Wales'. The original mansion is long since demolished, but the coach house is now the Welsh residence of the Prince of Wales (I wonder what Prince Charles thinks about the pipeline). The estate itself has several tantalising connections with the Physicians of Myddfai – indeed, the name itself means 'Grove of Wormwood', and wormwood was once regarded as an important disinfectant.

Over the years, the true history of the Physicians of Myddfai has become inextricably linked with the legend of the Lady of Llyn y Fan

*The view south-east from Pen y Bylchau, towards the clear felled pipeline route. The return journey follows an ancient track along the right side of the shallow valley just right of centre.*

Fach, a famous Welsh folk tale. According to the legend, the Physicians of Myddfai were the descendants of a beautiful fairy who appeared from Llyn y Fan Fach – a remote and tranquil lake, situated high on the Carmarthen Fan. This fairy was wooed by a local shepherd boy, and they eventually married and set up home at Esgair Llaethdy, a farm near the village of Myddfai, where they raised three sons. Following three 'unjust blows', the lady left her husband and returned to the depths of the lake, but before she went she taught her three sons the arts of healing and showed them where to find the necessary herbs, all of which grew in profusion in the area. According to one version of the legend, her eldest son was named Rhiwallon.

So much for the legend. What is certain is that, in the early thirteenth century, a man named Rhiwallon Feddyg was the personal physician of Rhys Gryg, Lord of Dinefwr and the warrior son of the Welsh Prince, Rhys ap Gruffydd. Rhiwallon had three sons, Cadwgan, Gruffydd and Einion,

*The onward route from spot height 429 – potentially tricky navigation!
The easiest route is to head directly towards the distant Carmarthen Fan,
following any of several paths. Resist the temptation to trend left! The best
defined path follows the upper (left) slopes of the valley to the right.*

and they and all their descendants became famous for their skill as doctors, not only in Wales, but throughout the UK and Europe. Their medical wisdom is recorded in *The Red Book of Hergest*, which dates back to the thirteenth century, and several of their original manuscripts are held in the British Museum. These show that their healing powers were based upon a materia medica of about 175 herbs, all of which grew locally, and many of which still thrive in the area. The last named 'Physician of Myddfai' died in 1842, and his tombstone lies in the porch of the village church.

From the trig point, continue along the centre of the ridge for just under 1.5 kilometres, walking parallel to the tilestone quarries, soon crossing a saddle en route for the next rise (spot height 429). It really is a delight to walk here – the nature of the terrain means that conditions underfoot are easy, the views are stunningly panoramic, and ravens, red kites and skylarks are your constant companions. You may also come across groups of hardy Welsh ponies. You eventually reach the area of the spot height, where the summit is marked by a low, stone post (marking the watershed between the Usk and the Towy), close to which are the scant remains of several more Bronze Age cairns.

The next section of the walk, although relatively straightforward, demands careful navigation, particularly if the visibility is none too good. The problem is that there is a plethora of paths from which to choose, not all of them heading in the right direction! What you must do is turn left (south), head downhill to the tilestone quarries, and then make for the mountain road that lies to the south, about 2 kilometres away. If the visibility is good, you will see, directly in front of you, the distant peaks of the Carmarthen Fan and, nearer at hand, several paths heading across the moor. Slightly to the right is a deep valley, the rightmost path heading along the left side of this before disappearing around a low spur. Ideally, you should cut across the hillside to reach this rightmost path. This leads directly to the mountain road, reaching it at Bylchau Blaenclydach, just to the east of Arhosfa'r Garreg-lwyd, the huge Roman marching camp mentioned earlier – although the remains of this are, sadly, becoming increasingly difficult to trace. Alternatively, you can follow either of the two paths that cross the higher ground to the left of the valley, heading directly towards the leftmost peak of the Carmarthen Fan and taking in some delightful if wild walking across the intervening low top of Fedw Fawr before reaching the road via Bryn Pwllygerwn. If the visibility is poor, however, and you cannot see the Carmarthen Fan, it may be prudent to use a compass, in which case you should follow a grid bearing of about 150° for approximately 2.5 kilometres.

Whichever route you choose, turn left when you reach the road, and follow it to an obvious bridge – Pont ar Wysg – the stream it crosses being the juvenile River Usk, the waters of which are captured by the Usk Reservoir only a short distance downstream. Continue across the cattle grid and along the road as it plunges into a dense conifer plantation, then take the first lane to the left, following the tarmac for just under 2 kilometres to reach the Usk Reservoir dam.

The Usk Reservoir lies at an altitude of just over 300 metres, and has supplied Swansea with water since 1955. The earth and concrete dam, 480 metres long and 30 metres high, took five years to build at a cost of £3 million, and captures the headwaters of the River Usk and the Nant Henwen in a reservoir with a surface area of 118 hectares and a capacity of some 4 billion litres. So much for the statistics! Most people simply know it for its trout fishing and the abundant wildlife that lives around its shores. It is a popular beauty spot that attracts many visitors.

Walk across the dam and turn left along the lane at the far end, soon passing a slipway and a hut where you can buy fishing permits. After about 300 metres, just before a picnic area, turn right on to a gated forestry track and start to climb away from the reservoir. Keep straight on along the main track all the way to the top of the hill where you emerge from the forestry, close to the shame of the pipeline. Continue straight ahead to reach a T-junction, and then turn right to reach a hill gate, beyond which is an ancient track that takes you back towards Pen y Bylchau. It is along this section that the full effect of the pipeline becomes obvious – it's not simply that laying the pipeline has ripped up the ground (which it has), it's equally as evident (and as disgraceful) that the once open moorland is now divided into sections by a series of fenced corridors, which look awful. Few people will dispute that the pipeline has had a hugely detrimental effect upon this ancient and fragile landscape.

To your right, as you follow the track, is Waun Ddu – the Black Bog – a raised bog and a Site of Special Scientific Interest. Although the pipeline cleverly skirts the boundary of the SSSI, I fail to see how it cannot have affected the local drainage in some way, which leads me to believe that it must be having an effect on the bog. As you make your away across this section, it is worth considering that, with the exception of the pipeline, the terrain has probably changed little since the Romans marched across it – which gives you a far more realistic perspective of the Roman invasion than simply reading about it in a book!

Once at Pen y Bylchau, the obvious saddle in the ridge ahead, turn right on to the grassy track (or climb back on to the ridge), and return to the Roman road near Y Pigwn, from where it is a simple matter to retrace your steps to the parking area.

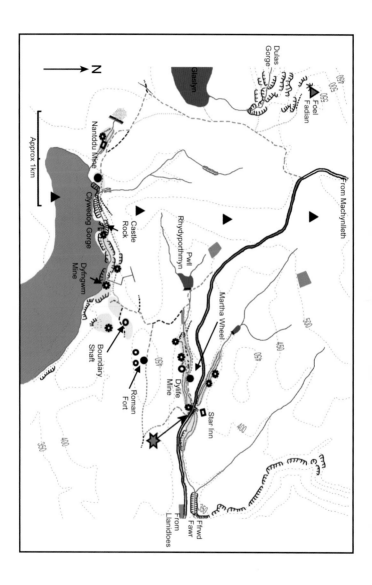

N

Approx 1km

Dulas Gorge

Glaslyn

Foel Fadian

From Machynlleth

Nantddu Mine

Clywedog Gorge

Castle Rock

Dyfngwm Mine

Pwll Rhydyporthmyn

Martha Wheel

Boundary Shaft

Roman Fort

Dylife Mine

Star Inn

From Llanidloes

Ffrwd Fawr

500
450
450
500
550
400
400
350
350
450

160

# 9.
# A LEGACY OF LEAD

A stunningly scenic look at the huge but largely forgotten lead mining industry of mid-Wales, visiting the site of one of the largest waterwheels in Europe, and several remarkably remote remains. The walk also takes you past two magnificent but seldom visited, hidden gorges, and follows a short section of Owen Glyndwr's Way.

## BACKGROUND INFORMATION

**Location** Dylife, on the mountain road between Llanidloes and Machynlleth.

**Start & finish point** Large, rough lay-by at SN861939, just opposite the lane leading to The Star Inn.

**Maps needed** OS Explorer 215.

**Map distance** 12 kilometres.

**Height gain** 270 metres.

**Terrain** Reasonable paths and tracks for the most part, including one section along a quiet mountain road. However, a short section at the head of Nant Twymyn (Dylife Ravine) can be very muddy and overgrown, and any exploration of the Clywedog Gorge will involve sometimes indistinct paths on loose and potentially dangerous ground. Both these sections are avoidable.

**Duration** Allow 4 hours plus exploration time.

**Hazards** Deep mine shafts, some of which are unfenced; deep, steep sided gorges with plenty of loose material and sudden, unexpected drops; unstable masonry around ruined mine buildings.

**Public transport** This walk is fairly remote, the nearest bus routes being at Llanidloes and Machynlleth. The nearest train stations are at Caersws and Machynlleth.

**Amenities/facilities** There are few amenities at Dylife apart from The Star Inn. The nearest settlements with any reasonable facilities are Llanbrynmair, Llanidloes, and Machynlleth.

DESPITE THEIR POPULAR IMAGE, the lonely hills of Central Wales are not quite as unspoiled as many people believe. Visitor attractions such as the Llywernog Silver Lead Mine on the A44 east of Aberystwyth, and the Bryntail and Fan Lead Mines near Llanidloes, suggest that farming has not always been the main industry hereabouts, and no one who has followed the spectacular mountain road between Devil's Bridge and Rhayader can have failed to be impressed by the remains of the vast Cwmystwyth Mine. Indeed, mining for silver, copper and, particularly, for lead has been a major influence throughout the region, affecting both society and landscape.

Lying towards the northern edge of what industrial archaeologists call the Central Wales Orefield, the tiny settlement of Dylife is not exactly a tourist hot spot. Those who do come here are mainly just passing through, often at speed, following the splendid mountain road between Llanidloes and Machynlleth, although some stop at the large lay-by (a kilometre to the east of the village) in order to marvel at the spectacular Twymyn Gorge. Few who stop know that the distant roar of water which accompanies the view comes from Ffrwd Fawr, a stunning waterfall which plunges vertically down a 40-metre cliff to the left, and which can be seen only if you get as close to the wire fence as possible at the top end of the lay-by. Fewer still realise that Dylife was once a thriving village, the site of one of the largest lead mines in Wales, or that two even more spectacular gorges lie near by, both completely hidden from the road, and both arguably more impressive than that of the Twymyn. Both will be visited during this walk.

Flint arrowheads discovered hereabouts indicate that people have lived in this area since Stone Age times, and they almost certainly started to mine the more accessible minerals during the Bronze Age. The Romans mined here, too, building a furnace not far from The Star Inn to smelt the ore, and siting a fort on a hill overlooking the village in order to defend their interests and safeguard the valuable resources they were exploiting. Although little is known about these early mines, local enthusiasts have managed to trace a reasonably detailed mining history back as far as the seventeenth century, and among other things, this shows that, bolstered by advances in mining technology, production slowly increased over a period of about 150 years, reaching its peak in the boom years of the nineteenth century. For almost a century, the Welsh lead industry prospered; Dylife Mine grew to become one of the largest producers of lead in Europe, and for a time, Wales was a world leader in the production of the metal. But it was not to last. As cheap imports began to arrive, first from Spain, then from the USA and even Australia, so the Welsh metal mining industry went into terminal decline. Mining finally ceased at Dylife in 1901, although there was sporadic reworking of the spoil heaps over the following three decades, and huge amounts of stone were excavated from the spoil heaps during the construction of the dam at the nearby Llyn Clywedog Reservoir. Indeed, the brick-built weighbridge situated just below the bank opposite the parking area dates from this period, and has no connection whatsoever with the lead mines.

Dylife today is a mere remnant of what it once was. In 1857, over 1,000 people lived in the village, and there were two chapels and a church, a school and school house, a vicarage, three inns, and ninety-two houses. The three original mines (Esgairgaled, Llechwedd Ddu and Dylife), were by this time worked by one company and became jointly known as Dylife Mine, and more houses were built over the following twenty years as the mine continued to be successful. Dylife was, indeed, a thriving community. There was a grocery and a butcher, a post office and a smithy, and a monthly fair was attended by shoemakers from Llanbrynmair as well as other traders from Llanidloes and Machynlleth. There was also a cockpit – a popular place of entertainment at the time – where wages were wagered.

How different it is today. Following the decline and closure of the mines at the start of the twentieth century, people began to move away, there being no other work in the area. The resulting decay has been remarkably rapid and dramatic. The mine buildings are long gone, most of them having been

*Ffrwd Fawr from the lay-by on the approach to Dylife village.*

demolished in 1911, and many of the houses have disappeared, the stones from which they were built now scattered and overgrown, a part of the landscape once again. It has taken a remarkably short period of time for the works of man to revert to nature, and it is difficult for the untrained eye to recognise what has happened here. Visit this area in the company of an experienced industrial archaeologist and you will be amazed. I am no expert, so my background notes can only give you a taste of the amazing heritage, but I hope they will add something to the atmosphere of this place as you wend your way.

From the rough lay-by opposite The Star Inn, the mountain road to Machynlleth snakes up towards the horizon. The main route joins this road a little later, so you can, if you wish, follow the tarmac all the way to the track leading to Glaslyn, but it is far more interesting (if more rough and muddy) to walk upstream alongside the Twymyn through the surface remains of the lead mine. To do this, walk a short distance along the road with The Star Inn to your right, pass the post box, cross the ravaged ravine,

*The Dylife Ravine. Rhod Goch (Martha Wheel) was situated behind the scant ruin, just visible on the track to the right of centre. Its water supply leat is the obvious level line to the left.*

and go through the first gate on the left. Below and to your left is the site of the dressing floor, where the rough ore was once literally pummelled into a useable state, and where the youthful Twymyn stream disappears under the road through a mined passage. Continue along the right side of the Dylife ravine, following a good track alongside a fence, soon reaching a fenced area where there are the scant remains of a building and a long rectangular hole – the remains of a large waterwheel pit. This is the site of Rhod Goch (the Red Wheel), more commonly known as Martha Wheel. Erected in 1851, this predominantly wooden waterwheel had a diameter of 63 feet (just over 19 metres), and was 3½ feet (about 1 metre) wide, making it the largest waterwheel in mainland Britain, and one of the largest in Europe. The wheel was used to power the pumps that drained water from the mines, and to haul ore from two nearby shafts, one of which lies next to the mountain road, the other of which you will see shortly. It is said that, once erected, the wheel turned ceaselessly for more than fifty years.

On leaving the site of Martha Wheel, make your way carefully down the steep embankment to the river bed, dry in all but the wettest weather, and follow this upstream (to the right). A short distance away, off to the left, lies the obvious, open entrance to the Llechwedd Ddu Engine Shaft, with parts of the pumping rod and the shaft head frame still in place. Take care here as the ground around the shaft is loose and slippery, and an unplanned descent is not

*Rhod Goch waterwheel pit.*

*The Llechwedd Ddu Engine Shaft and Great Dylife Adit.*

to be recommended! Above, beyond and to the right, lies the yawning mouth of the Great Dylife Adit, the impressive main entrance to this section of the mine.

It is difficult for us to appreciate what life must have been like for these miners. Conditions underground were very hard, although the workers here were luckier than most, because in 1861, Dylife was the only mine in Wales where there were changing rooms for the miners. The long hours of gruelling work inevitably took their toll, but the worst problem was the lack of ventilation and the amount of dust. The very nature of the material being mined was also detrimental to health, and lead poisoning was endemic, not just among the miners, but also among the surface workers. The headstones in the local graveyard show that life expectancy was less than forty years.

Although there are several interesting remains further upstream, the onward route through the ravine beyond is effectively blocked by a picturesque cascade, so it is better to retrace your steps towards Martha Wheel, crossing the fence at the top of the embankment using the obvious stile. Turn left and walk alongside the fence and through a gate, then continue along a much grassier track along the right side of the valley. Do not climb to the next gate (usually open), but descend into the valley to reach a small platform of spoil, then continue on a faint path along the right bank of the stream – usually horribly boggy. Persevere, and you will soon come to a rickety stile, fairly obvious on the far side of the stream

*The far end of the Dylife Ravine. The way on is over a stile in the fence that crosses the stream, then up the left side of the valley beyond.*

where the fences meet. Cross both the stream and the stile, then fight your way up the gully beyond, keeping fairly close to the fence to your right, eventually emerging at a good track near a house. The remains of the leat which once supplied Martha Wheel with water can be seen as a horizontal scar running along the far side of the valley to your right. Bear right along the track, and follow it into the valley, past a dam on the left, which holds back the waters of Pwll Rhydyporthmyn (the reservoir built to supply water to Martha Wheel), then continue up the track to reach the mountain road from Dylife to Machynlleth, where you should bear left.

After just over a kilometre of steady ascent and increasingly expansive views, an obvious lake – Glaslyn – appears ahead and to the left, with the peaks of Plynlimon (or Pumlumon, to give it its correct name) as a backdrop. From most directions, Pumlumon appears as a boringly rounded mountain mass, but from here the peaks are surprisingly shapely. A short distance further and you reach a small parking area with a modern sculpted cycle-route milepost, where a track on the left is signposted with

*The distant peaks of Plynlimon from the mountain road.*

a duck! Turn left over the cattle grid, and follow the rough track towards the Glaslyn Nature Reserve, meandering to avoid large puddles after wet weather. After about a kilometre, the track joins Glyndwr's Way, which merges from the right.

Glyndwr's Way is one of three Welsh National Trails (as opposed to Long Distance Footpaths, of which there are currently nineteen). Opened in 2002, it meanders from Knighton to Welshpool via Machynlleth (where, in 1404, Owain Glyndwr held the first Welsh parliament), and passes several of the battlefields where Glyndwr and his army fought the English. A worthy National Trail it may be, but as you will soon see, it is not the busiest of paths, and sections of it are not at all well defined.

To your right at the junction is the spectacular Dulas Gorge – although there is little sign of it from the path. The easiest way to get a good view is to walk back along Glyndwr's Way for about 500 metres until you are above Creigiau Esgairfochnant on the slopes of Foel Fadian. The best view, however, is far more difficult to attain, as it involves heading due west across the often boggy heather moorland to reach a viewpoint looking straight down the gorge towards Machynlleth. Access to this viewpoint is now even more difficult than before, owing to the presence of a new barbed-wire fence – put in place, no doubt, to prevent unwary walkers from taking an unplanned shortcut to the bottom of the gorge!

*The spectacular Dulas Gorge, totally hidden from the road.*

Beyond the junction, the path continues towards Glaslyn, forking just before a cattle grid. The track on the right leads to a viewpoint overlooking the lake, where there is an information board giving details about the nature reserve and the long-term work being done here by the Montgomeryshire Wildlife Trust. Your onward journey, however, lies along the track straight ahead, over the cattle grid. Just beyond the next rise there is an indicator post which tells you that Glyndwr's Way veers off to the left, following a very indistinct path across the bog! Do not be too downhearted: this area is now Access Land, and the Right to Roam legislation means that you no longer have to bog-trot in order to continue. While you can squelch across the bog if you wish, it is far more pleasant to continue along the track for a further 500 metres to where it forks, just before a gate, then veer off to the left along an equally good if slightly more grassy track. At the point where the grassy track becomes rocky again, the remains of a dam can be seen off to the right, the flat, boggy ground on the nearside being all that remains of a reservoir that once supplied water to Dyfngwm Mine – more of which anon. The official line of Glyndwr's Way emerges from the bog to the left, just beyond which there is another fork where you should bear right, soon passing close to an old mine on the right.

Very little is known about this mine. Variously known as Cafarthfa (or Cyfarthfa) Copper Mine and Nantddu Lead Mine, it is thought it was worked for both lead and copper from about 1840. There are several remains here, including the inevitable spoil heap, a couple of shafts, several adits, and a waterwheel pit, the water for which was taken from Glaslyn, much to the annoyance of the woollen factories near Machynlleth, who also used the water from the lake. Indeed, the dispute over this water supply ended up in the Court of Chancery in 1880, since when the mine has been deserted. The whole site invites exploration, but be careful if you stray from the path anywhere in this area, as there are several open shafts and deep pits hidden in the vegetation.

Having explored, continue along the track which soon starts to descend past some corrugated iron farm buildings, built on the site of

*The onward route from Glaslyn towards the Clywedog Gorge.*

the Nantddu Mine mill, where there is a superb waterwheel pit. Cross a stile (or go through the permanently open gate), then descend towards the Clywedog Gorge on a less well-defined but well-signed path, passing extensive tailings from the mill, and then dropping steeply in a spectacular position to reach a modern wooden footbridge. Cross the bridge and climb the steep path on the far side, soon reaching a post with an acorn waymark. Veer off to the right, following a less well-defined, grassy path that runs along the edge of the magnificent gorge, the views becoming more spectacular with each step. The obvious prominence of Castle Rock (effectively, a huge lump of ore) dominates the near distance on the opposite side of the gorge, while on the near side, it is easy to make out the line of the leat that carried water from the reservoir above to the machinery of Dyfngwm Mine, which lies in the base of the gorge ahead. Keep your eyes open for the eyehole, carved to allow the leat to pass through a rock buttress opposite Castle Rock, and for adit entrances along the base of Castle Rock itself.

Cross a stile and continue along the path, rocky in places, being cautious of large drops on the right, the views along and down into the gorge becoming more impressive almost with every step. The tailings of Dyfngwm Mine are soon abundantly obvious along the base and left side of the gorge, and the dark mouth of an adit can be seen in the distance, at about the same

*The modern footbridge at the start of the Clywedog Gorge, built to carry Glyndwr's Way across the stream.*

*The superb Clywedog Gorge. The huge lump of rock at the bottom of the picture is the appropriately named Castle Rock. The Dyfngwm Mine water supply leat is obvious along the left side of the gorge.*

level as the path. Head for this adit, eventually veering right at a junction and dropping to the entrance, high above the gorge. This trial, driven in about 1850, is associated with the Dyfngwm Mine below.

Lead was almost certainly mined from the Clywedog Gorge in Roman times, and perhaps even earlier, the earliest workings being clustered around Castle Rock. However, the busiest period of exploitation began in the early 1700s, and Dyfngwm was an important mine. Although not as productive as Dylife, the two mines were closely linked (literally – as in latter years it was possible to walk underground from the one to the other) and, to some extent, they shared similar fortunes. However, whereas mining at Dylife ended in 1901, mining at Dyfngwm ended in the 1870s because the company that owned the mine were German (under the directorship of a Colonel Stronsberg), and they left Britain because of the Franco-Prussian War. Unlike Dylife, this closure was not the end of the story, for in 1931 the mine was bought by Hirnant Minerals, the same company that had been reworking the spoil tips at Dylife. The old roads and tracks were repaired, a new tramroad was constructed, and new buildings were erected, including a sizeable concentrating plant driven by a massive diesel engine. Even larger diesel engines were installed to provide compressed air to power hoists and boring drills, and the mind boggles at the thought of the difficulties of installing such huge engines in such a deep and remote location!

After its latest lease of life, the mine eventually closed again in 1935 following the death of its owner. Although the manager was retained for a further year to look after the mine, the price of lead meant that it was uneconomic to form a new company, and Dyfngwm was sold to a Sheffield company for dismantling. Despite this, and no doubt helped by its remoteness and the difficulty of access, many fine surface features still survive, and the whole site is now scheduled as an ancient monument. You could easily spend a whole day here simply wandering and wondering, but such exploration is beyond the scope of this book. If you do decide to explore further, take great care as there are many hidden pitfalls.

Follow the path beyond the adit entrance, fairly level to begin with and

*The trial adit at the top of the Clywedog Gorge, above Dyfngwm Mine.*

quite rocky, soon trending downhill and heading towards the left side of the spoil ahead, eventually reaching a modern wire fence, which marks the end of the access land. When I visited here while researching this walk, this fence blocked the public right of way, but I have been assured by Powys County Council that a new stile is to be built, so use this to cross the fence and then head towards the obvious shallow valley ahead. Trend left along the near side of the valley to reach a grassy track, which you follow to the left to reach a junction with a rockier track. There are many remains around here, all associated with either Dyfngwm or Dylife mine, or both. Indeed, near the strange 'box' (the back of an old van), further down the rocky track to the right, a fenced area keeps unwary travellers away from Boundary Shaft, part of Dylife mine. At just over 300 metres deep, this was (and still is) the deepest mine shaft in mid-Wales.

Do not go right towards the old van, but carry on along the track straight ahead, shortly reaching a waymarked bridal gate where Owen Glyndwr's Way rejoins from the left. Continue straight on along the gravelly track, which soon reaches a gate (usually open), and starts to descend. The track then swings round to the left and meets another gate, at which point you should turn right on to a muddier track and start to head uphill alongside a fence (to your left). Pass the next gate via a stile, shortly arriving at a television aerial on top of Pen y Crochben – obviously a booster for someone living in the valley!

According to a local story, a blacksmith by the name of Siôn Jones arrived in Dylife in 1725 looking for work. He came from Ystumtuen, a less productive lead mining area in Cardiganshire, and he left behind him his wife and two children. Several weeks passed by, and having heard nothing from him, his now worried wife travelled to Dylife with the children to make sure her husband was okay. It was a difficult journey involving a coach trip to Glan Dyfi, then a long walk over the mountains to Pen Dylife. She finally tracked her husband down to Felin Newydd, a house about 2 kilometres to the east of the Pen Dylife works. On the surface, Siôn seemed happy to see them, but the truth was that he had begun an affair with a maid from the nearby Llwyn y gog farm. After less than a week, Siôn's wife and family departed for Ystumtuen, accompanied by Siôn, but on a lonely stretch of track near the top of Pen Dylife, he murdered all three of them, and threw their bodies down a nearby disused mine shaft. He then returned to Felin Newydd, telling everyone that his wife and children had returned to Ystumtuen. He may even have got away with murder – except that the bodies were found, by chance, almost three months later, when men were sent to retrieve some timbers from the mine shaft.

On hearing that the bodies had been discovered, Siôn flew into a panic and ran to the nearby Clywedog Gorge where he tried to throw himself off Castle Rock into a pool below. His attempt at suicide was thwarted by some miners from the nearby Dyfngwm Mine, and he was taken to Welshpool where he stood trial and was found guilty of three murders. Not only was he sentenced to death, but he was taken back to Dylife where he was given his last job as a blacksmith – to make his own hanging frame. Gallows were built at Pen y Crochben, near where he committed the murders and not far from the shaft into which he threw the bodies. He was strapped into the iron frame, lifted on to horseback, a noose was put around his neck and the horse made to walk on. His body was left hanging for several years, and the pool below Castle Rock is known to this day as Llyn Siôn y glo.

A fanciful tale? Perhaps not, for in the late 1930s, very close to the site of the television aerial, two local men unearthed pieces of a gibbet, an iron cage and a skull – now exhibited at the Welsh Folk Museum at St Fagan's. There are also several reports of ghostly sightings in the area – some of a headless figure who used to descend a local shaft, frightening the miners, and others concerning the figure of a woman who would disappear if approached.

Continue along the track past the television aerial, very soon passing an area of obviously disturbed ground on the right. This marks the site of the Roman fortlet that was built to guard the lead mines, and considering it is nigh on 2,000 years old, it is remarkably well-preserved – the rectangular shape is very evident, enclosed by low earth banks, as is the entrance. Go through the gate beyond the fortlet, and stay on the well-defined, grassy track, which runs along the top of the ridge with panoramic views to either side. Immediately after the next gate, turn left on to another grassy but muddier track heading down into the valley, the surface improving as you descend. You will shortly see The Star Inn in the distance on the far side of the valley, and the track leads you almost directly back to the start.

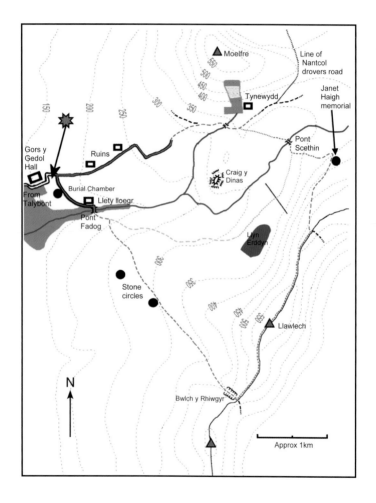

Moelfre

Line of Nantcol drovers road

Tynewydd

Janet Haigh memorial

Gors y Gedol Hall

Ruins

Pont Scethin

Craig y Dinas

From Talybont

Burial Chamber

Llety lloegr

Pont Fadog

Llyn Erddyn

Stone circles

N

Llawlech

Bwlch y Rhiwgyr

Approx 1km

# 10.
# THE ROVING DROVERS

*A lonely sojourn through seldom visited countryside, following forgotten tracks in the wake of the cattle masters of mid-Wales. Some of the paths are ancient, and there are several interesting archaeological sites en route. The main route includes an ascent of Llawlech, with superb panoramic views, although this can be avoided.*

## BACKGROUND INFORMATION

**Location** Near Dyffryn Ardudwy, on the A496 between Barmouth and Harlech.

**Start & finish point** Rough car park (£1 honesty box) at SH602230, at the end of Ffordd Gors, the long, straight drive to Gors y Gedol Hall.

**Maps needed** OS Explorer OL18.

**Map distance** 12 kilometres.

**Height gain** 500 metres.
This can be reduced to 8 kilometres with 220 metres of ascent by avoiding the ascent of Llawlech.

**Terrain** Generally reasonable paths and tracks, although some sections can be extremely boggy, and the paths over Llawlech are loose and rocky in places.

**Duration** Allow 5 hours.

**Hazards** The route finding around Pont Scethin can be tricky in misty conditions, and the terrain on this section is extremely boggy during or after wet weather. Normal mountain safety precautions should be taken on Llawlech.

**Public transport** There are railway stations at Tyddyn Goronwy (Talybont) and Llanenddwyn (Dyffryn Ardudwy), and two bus routes travel through Talybont between Barmouth and Maentwrog.

**Amenities/facilities** Harlech and Barmouth have all the amenities one associates with popular holiday destinations, although some are seasonal.

WAY BACK IN THE FOURTEENTH CENTURY, during the reign of Edward III, the constables of the Welsh castles received a message from the king ordering them to buy up all the cattle in their area and have them driven to London, Southampton and Dover in order to feed the troops involved in the Hundred Years War. The king's father,

Edward II (the first English prince to be given the title Prince of Wales), had earlier sent officials to Wales to buy cattle to feed the household troops at Windsor Castle, and records suggest that the trading of live meat between Wales and England was well established by this time. Indeed, recent research indicates a flourishing cattle trade as early as the mid-thirteenth century, which suggests that the origins of the trade go back into the Dark Ages. Whatever its origins, by the mid-seventeenth century the export of livestock, particularly cattle, was one of the primary sources of Welsh revenue.

To cite a few examples, records show that 10,000 cattle were exported from Anglesey in 1794. By the start of the nineteenth century, over 14,000 'Welsh runts' were being sent annually to the Midlands from Anglesey and the Lleyn Peninsula, while as many as 30,000 head of cattle were being driven through mid-Wales to Hereford.

Although the main livestock comprised Welsh Black cattle, these drives (or droves) often included sheep, pigs, geese and even turkeys. Because they had to arrive at their destination in reasonable condition, ready for fattening prior to being sent to market, the pace of the drives was fairly gentle, the average speed being about 3 kilometres an hour. Thus drives from Tregaron to Warwickshire took over a fortnight, while the journey from North Wales to Kent took over three weeks. Additionally, most if not all the animals were shod for the journey, the cattle wearing iron shoes or 'cues', the pigs wearing woollen boots with a leather sole, and the birds having their feet covered in a mixture of tar and sand. Driving the large herds of animals was an extremely skilled job, and the drovers often used dogs to help them. The most popular breed was the corgi, because the dogs were hard working, and big enough to nip the heels of tardy animals, yet small enough to avoid the resultant kick! They were also amazingly intelligent, and would often find their own way home, arriving back in mid-Wales before the men. Indeed, in some areas, tradition has it that the women would only start to get ready for the return of their droving menfolk when the dogs reappeared.

The drovers themselves were a tough lot, and were not particularly popular with farmers. There are several reasons for this, the main one being that they often bought the livestock on credit, promising to return with the money once they had sold the animals at the English markets. This system was obviously open to abuse, and while the majority of drovers were honest, there were a few villains, and the situation was fraught with risk until the founding of the Drovers Banks in the late eighteenth century. Furthermore, the movement of such a large group of animals could cause havoc in the areas through which it was travelling, and local farmers would hurry to lock up their livestock as soon as they heard the noisy approach of a drove, for if their animals got caught up in it, it was unlikely that they would ever see them again.

On the other hand, not only were the drovers extremely skilled, but they were also often the only source of information about the world at large. Additionally, they had to be tough because of the nature of their work. In order to avoid tolls and unnecessary disruption, they tended to avoid main roads and turnpikes, instead following ancient tracks and even old Roman roads. This made their journeys extremely hazardous, not just because of the nature of the terrain and the weather through the Welsh mountains, but also because wolves were a common threat until the eighteenth century. More dangerous, however, were the bands of armed brigands who knew that drovers often carried large amounts of money.

It was the advent of the railway that slowly killed the drovers. Livestock movements were easier, safer and quicker by rail, and as the rail network grew, so a way of life began to fade, eventually to disappear altogether. Since that time, many of the old routes have fallen into disuse and become lost, while others have been used as the basis for modern roads and are now buried beneath tarmac. For example, if you are driving through the wilds of Wales and find yourself on a lane with wide verges and walls or hedges set well back, the likelihood is that you are following a route once used by the drovers.

So much for the history – now for the practicalities. The route taken by this walk follows a variety of tracks of different ages, and allows you to come face-to-face with some of the problems met by the drovers. To get to the start, follow the long, straight lane – Ffordd Gors – which heads east from the A496 Barmouth to Harlech road, starting almost directly opposite the chapel at the northern edge of Talybont. At the far end, do not go through the gates of Gors y Gelog Hall (a well-preserved sixteenth-century manor house, currently under private ownership), but follow the lane around to the right of the buildings, eventually reaching

*Looking along the walled track towards Moelfre. The origins of this ancient track are lost in the mists of time, and the original paved surface is now buried beneath more modern metalling.*

a rough parking area on the right (£1 honesty box), just before the lane ends at a gate.

On leaving the car park, turn right and go straight ahead through two gates, heading slightly uphill along a rough, walled track (ignore the gate and the tarmac lane on the right, immediately beyond the car park, along which you will eventually return). The views, particularly of the coast, are good right from the start, and the ruins of several abandoned farmsteads add atmosphere. Although the track is now used as the access route to the Llyn Bodlyn Reservoir, its origins are far more ancient, as indicated by the dry stone walls to either side. Sadly, much of the original paved surface, still very much in evidence thirty years ago, has now been destroyed. In addition to being the access route to several long ruined farms, the track was almost certainly used by drovers travelling between Bron-y-foel and Bwlch y Rhiwgyr, and it may also have been used as a link between Gors y Gedol Hall and the Harlech to London coach road ahead, but its origins are now lost in the mists of time. The route is obvious, the walking easy, and the views increasingly expansive, and there are ruins of varying ages to either side.

Something that becomes increasingly apparent as you journey up the valley, away from civilisation, is the lack of noise or, perhaps more correctly, the presence of silence. On still winter days in particular, there is a wealth of nothing – no birdsong, no wind noise, hardly any water noise at this level of the track – just a brooding silence that is almost oppressive. Granted, the effect is sometimes spoiled by the sudden reverberating roar of a low-flying fast jet, but the echoes quickly clear to leave a profound sense of silent emptiness. You may well find yourself humming or singing in order to give your ears something to do. What a difference to only a couple of centuries ago, for when the drovers were passing through, the valley would have been filled with sound, the shouts and cries of the men and the noise of the animals, reverberating between the opposing mountainsides.

Some 800 metres beyond the second of two sharp bends, the track escapes from its bounding walls and heads more openly across the hillside, curving to the right to reach the top of the small spur that has so far obscured much of the onward view. It is here that another track merges from the left, and you join the route of the Harlech to London coach road – a route that you will follow along an unlikely line for the next 2 kilometres or so. Continue to the top of the rise to reach a yellow waymark where the track curves slightly to the left. The coach road continues as a muddy, less well-defined path that branches off to the right at this point, but it is worth continuing

*The scant ruins of Tynewydd, once an inn, sheltering beneath the slopes of Moelfre.*

along the reservoir track for a short distance until you are level with the far end of the patch of conifers to your left. Beyond the slight rise, nestling at the base of the hillside, lie the scant ruins of Tynewydd, once an inn. Whether this was a coaching inn or a drovers inn (or both) is unclear, but a welcoming inn it certainly once was, and local legend has it that it was the site of several raids by the bands of armed bandits that roamed the area. Drovers reached this spot from the Nantcol Valley, on the far side of Moelfre (the mountain immediately to the north) along a drovers road that crossed the saddle between Moelfre and Y Llethr (further east). This is shown on OS maps as a bridleway, but is now very difficult to follow. As you gaze at the terrain, try to imagine what it must have been like to drive herds of cattle, sheep and pigs, along with flocks of geese and turkeys, across such terrain, in all weathers, and without the benefit of modern clothing or technology.

Retrace your steps to the waymark, following the route taken by the Nantcol drovers, and then turn back left on to a much less well-defined and muddy path, heading almost directly towards a low, rocky outcrop in the base of the valley ahead. At the far end of the rocky spur to your right is Craig y Dinas, an Iron Age hill fort that, considering its age, is better preserved than the 'road' along which you are currently walking, the surface of which has either sunk into the bog or been washed away by the countless ribbons of water making their way towards the bottom of the valley. If you did not know it was there, you would have difficulty in recognising your route as a road, but every now and then, you reach a section where you get the feeling that, just maybe, you are following the route of something more substantial . . . a low embankment, a few laid slabs, a fallen marker stone, the suggestion of a cutting. And then, in the base of the valley, a strange arrangement of stones resolves itself into the low retaining walls of a bridge – the enigmatic Pont Scethin – a bridge in the middle of nowhere. Getting to it, though, is not straightforward, as the coach road deteriorates once more into a boggy wallow. Give it another twenty years and it will have disappeared altogether... and another small snippet of living history will have faded forever from human experience.

Pont Scethin itself is delightful – a narrow, low, hump-backed stone bridge of obvious antiquity, crossing the Ysgethin stream in the midst of a lonely valley. Yet this was the crossing used by the important coach

*ABOVE* The easy-to-miss junction near Tynewydd. The path to Pont Scethin bears off to the right through the sedge, initially heading towards the low outcrop of rocks in the base of the valley (just to the right of the post).

*RIGHT* Pont Scethin – a bridge in the middle of nowhere.

road linking Harlech and London, and I find the thought of a stagecoach pulled by four horses rattling across it quite amazing! I wonder what went through the minds of the travellers as they passed this way. Did they look at the landscape with wonder or dread? Or did they keep their eyes tightly closed for the entire, awful journey?

On the far side of the bridge, the coach road bears off to the right and then meanders gently up the boggy lower slopes of Llawlech. Thankfully, the path here is marked by a line of laid slabs which runs for a significant distance, and even though several of the flagstones have sunk just below the surface of the bog and are now, therefore, just below the level of the water, it is possible to gain relatively dry access to the more grassy slopes above. Having left the slabs behind, keep your eyes open for an old marker stone – an obvious upright boulder to the left of the path, with a more modern, low wooden post driven into the ground alongside it.

To shorten the walk and avoid the ascent of Llawlech, head off to the right from near this marker stone, following what is initially an ill-defined and very boggy path, which gets better the further you go, eventually passing through an obvious gap in a substantial stone wall. This is almost certainly the route taken by a majority of the drovers, many of whom would have wished to avoid driving their livestock up and over Llawlech at this point, heading instead towards a lower and more gentle route through Bwlch y Rhiwgyr. The track soon runs along the northern shores of Llyn Erddyn, then meanders across the open hillside to rejoin the main route just before Pont Fadog.

Beyond the marker stone, the coach road curves to the left and begins to angle its way up the hillside, its course becoming increasingly well-defined, and surprisingly well preserved in places. At one point there is an old Ordnance Survey benchmark carved into a stone slab on the surface of the path, and it is reasonable to suppose that this stone is therefore one of the original paving slabs. Beyond this, the track makes a sharp right turn in an attempt to find the easiest way up increasingly steep slopes, and just beyond the bend you reach a slate slab set into the upslope bank. This is a touching memorial to one Janet Haigh. The inscription, now rapidly weathering and increasingly difficult to read, says:

'Gogoniant i Dduw [trans = Glory to God]. To the enduring memory of Janet Haigh, who even as late as her eighty fourth year, despite dim

sight and stiffened joints, still loved to walk this way from Talybont to Penmaenpool. This stone was placed in 1953 by her son, Melvyn, sometime Bishop of Winchester.' It finishes with the words 'Courage, Traveller!'

Hats off to Janet Haigh, who must have been a remarkable woman to travel this way in her eighties, as the next kilometre involves a stiff climb on uncertain footing. Even though the surface of the track was undoubtedly in a better state of repair fifty years ago, the angle would not have been any less! Consider, too, the drovers and other users of this road. Although a majority of drovers would most likely have avoided this direct way over Llawlech, taking instead the less demanding route through Bwlch y Rhiwgyr to the west, what must it have been like for those people travelling between London and Harlech in a wooden wheeled coach pulled by four horses? With a very real threat from armed bandits in these hills, this was very much the British Wild West until late in the eighteenth century.

As you might expect, the higher you climb, the better become the views. To the west, the Irish Sea disappears into hazy distance, while slightly further north, the Lleyn Peninsula lies as a smudge across the horizon, with Yr Eifl, an obvious prominence, and Tremadog Bay and the Glaslyn Estuary, a sandy foreground. Almost due north, the saddle between Moelfre and Y Llethr frames the distant pyramid of Snowdon, while further right again, at the head of the Ysgethin valley, lies Diffwys and the southern slopes of the Rhinogs. Eventually, shortly beyond a stone

wall, the path levels, and as you reach the top of the ridge, the views expand again, and your gaze is drawn to the flats and meanders of the Mawddach Estuary, far below. As you slowly raise your eyes up the slopes beyond, they finally come to rest on the majestic bulk of Cadair Idris, dominating the magnificent mountains of mid-Wales.

The coach road continues through a gate in the amazing stone wall that runs the entire length of the Llawlech ridge, but your onward route lies to the right, alongside the nearside of the wall. Do not be tempted to climb the ladder stile to the right of the gate at this point, as you will be on the wrong side of the wall and will have difficulties later. Follow a faint but obvious path alongside the wall, the views still unfolding, soon reaching a ladder stile. Cross this, and continue straight ahead, following a reasonable path to the right of the wall, eventually crossing another ladder stile just before the obvious summit of Llawlech, which is a fine viewpoint. The stone wall – so incredible a structure that it should be regarded as a work of art – continues unabated along the now descending ridge, and your route also continues alongside it, following a reasonably well-defined if sometimes slippery path. Drop steeply from the summit, climb over the next rise (which is not as bad as it looks when it first appears), then drop steeply again to reach Bwlch y Rhiwgyr, which is a gloomy spot in all but the brightest of weathers.

Bwlch y Rhiwgyr is the obvious hiatus along the Llawlech ridge. Visible for miles around, it has been used as a crossing point for millennia. Five thousand years ago, it was used by the Stone Age people, originally from Ireland, who were slowly moving southwards and eastwards in search of richer pastures, and to this day, the countryside to the north-west of the pass is littered with ancient cairns, standing stones, hut circles, stone circles, and burial chambers, as you will shortly see. More recently, a medieval road ran this way, and even the earliest drovers were quick to see its value. But it was also a dangerous road, for the mountains were full of perils both natural and human, and the pass would have been the ideal spot for an ambush. With this in mind, it is probable that the drovers from the Nantcol Valley joined forces with those from Bron-y-foel to make the crossing, believing that there was safety in numbers.

Arriving at the pass, turn right and walk through the narrow defile, following the line of the medieval road towards the distant Lleyn Peninsula. The path, good to begin with, soon deteriorates and becomes loose, rocky and awkward – in wet weather, it is little better than a stream. The onward route is obvious in the distance, running alongside (and to the right of) the wall, and the footing improves once you reach the base

*Cadair Idris from the summit of Llawlech.*

*Bwlch y Rhiwgyr is the only hiatus along the high ridge of Llawlech, and was an obvious choice for a crossing point. The drovers road is the green ribbon through the bouldery ground, heading from left to right alongside the wall.*

of the pass, although it can still be unpleasantly boggy after wet spells. The further you go, the more well-preserved becomes the track – there are bridges made from huge stone slabs, and the occasional paved section. You are also surrounded by ancient history, a good example of which is close to the path. Immediately after a section where the ancient wall on the left has been replaced by a modern wire fence, and just past a ladder stile where the wall reappears, there are two stone circles in the field to the left, built from low stone slabs set on end. Neither are 'in your face' stone circles such as you find at Stonehenge or Avebury, but I find them impressive, nonetheless; a visible link to our ancient past. Whether they were religious or social sites, or were used for some other purpose, is unknown.

There are new fences in this area, recent enough not to be shown on my map, but the route is clear – an obvious path through the boulders, with occasional gates and ladder stiles. Continue straight ahead for some distance, first to the right of the wall, then across the open hillside, eventually descending more steeply into the valley of the Ysgethin where you reach a junction with track which has a concrete gully to assist drainage, beyond which is a tarmac lane, which is followed all the way back to the start.

It is at this point that the shorter route, following the drovers road along the northern shores of Llyn Erddyn, rejoins the main route.

The lane leads gently downhill into the wooded base of the Ysgethin valley, soon reaching the stream, which is crossed by another magnificent stone bridge – Pont Fadog – which dates from 1762. If you search carefully you will find a stone inscribed with the date and the letters S A E R, which probably refer to the craftsman builder. Cross the bridge and continue up the lane on the far side, soon passing an old stone cottage on the left. This is Llety Lloegr – the English Lodgings – once an overnight shelter for the drovers. It was also the site of an emergency shoeing station, where any animals who had thrown their shoes could be re-shod in preparation for the difficult passage over the mountains ahead.

Continue along the lane, soon climbing out of the wooded confines of the valley and on to a gorse covered hillside, where the views open out again. Arrive here at the right time, and the sunsets across the Irish Sea are stunning. Perhaps that is why, in Bronze Age times, the site was chosen for a burial chamber, the capstone of which is obvious to the left of the road, just where it levels out. Little now remains of the Cors y Gedol burial chamber apart from the capstone which, according to local legend, was thrown here from Moelfre by King Arthur (hence the alternative name of King Arthur's Quoit). Believed to date from about 4000 BC, the chamber would originally have been much bigger. Indeed, there is evidence of a long mound about 26 metres long and 12 metres wide running west from the capstone, and there are also several standing stones (some now lying down!) in the immediate vicinity.

Having pondered the history of the chamber, continue along the lane, shortly reaching a gate. Go through this, turn left, and the car park is immediately on the left.

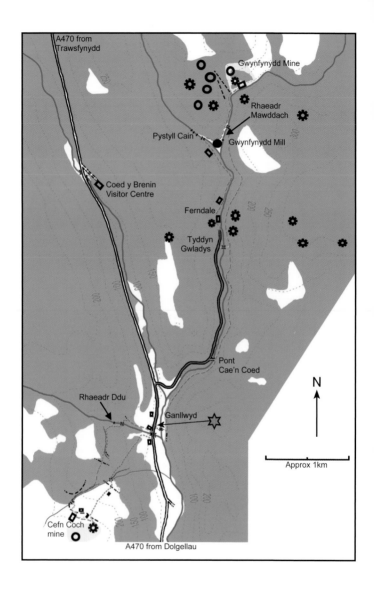

A470 from
Trawsfynydd

Gwynfynydd Mine

Rhaeadr
Mawddach

Pystyll Cain

Gwynfynydd Mill

Coed y Brenin
Visitor Centre

Ferndale

Tyddyn
Gwladys

Pont
Cae'n Coed

N

Rhaeadr Ddu

Ganllwyd

Approx 1km

Cefn Coch
mine

A470 from Dolgellau

# 11.
# GOLD FEVER

A wooded wander through a Welsh Klondike, now largely blanketed by the vast Coed y Brenin forest, with rushing torrents, magnificent waterfalls, and the atmospheric remains of several gold mines. The walk first explores the deep gorge of the Mawddach, then climbs through ancient oak woods on the opposite side of the valley, to gain spectacular views from the open slopes of the south-eastern Rhinogs. The first part of the walk makes a great outing on an otherwise wasted wet day.

## BACKGROUND INFORMATION

**Location** Coed y Brenin, just to the north of Dolgellau, in Southern Snowdonia.

**Start & finish point** Car park & picnic area at SH727243, in Ganllwyd, on the A470 north of Dolgellau.

**Maps needed** OS Explorer OL18.

**Map distance** 15 kilometres.

**Height gain** 330 metres.

The route can easily be split into two separate walks, the first of 10 kilometres with 130 metres of ascent, the second of 5 kilometres with 200 metres of ascent.

**Terrain** The first part of the walk is on lanes and good tracks throughout. The second part uses less well-trodden paths and has sections which are awkwardly slippery and boggy.

**Duration** Allow 5 hours (3 hours for the first part, and 2 hours for the second).

**Hazards** Hidden shafts and crumbling masonry around the old mines, particularly if you stray from the path. Speeding mountain bikes on the first part. Slippery rocks near the waterfalls, particularly on the second part.

**Public transport** Ganllwyd can be reached by bus from Dolgellau. The nearest railway stations are at Fairbourne and Barmouth.

**Amenities/facilities** There are public toilets in the Ganllwyd car park, and at the Coed y Brenin visitor centre (off the A470 just over 2 kilometres to the north of Ganllwyd), which also serves excellent refreshments. Dolgellau has all the facilities you would expect of a busy town.

GANLLWYD IS ONE OF THOSE PLACES you pass through rather than visit. Indeed, for many years I regularly drove through the village on my way to and from Snowdonia, without so much as a second glance – until, by chance, I happened to overhear a conversation about the old mines and waterfalls in the locality. My curiosity aroused, I consulted the map, with the result that the next time I journeyed that way, I did so leaving plenty of time to stop and explore. I have since been back many times, and while, undoubtedly, there is much I have yet to discover, the walk described here will introduce you to some of the more accessible fascinations of this area.

The village itself lies on the A470, the main north–south road through Wales, in what has become known as the Dolgellau gold belt – an arc of land between about 1.5 kilometres and 5 kilometres wide, which runs for almost 25 kilometres from the northern shores of the Mawddach Estuary, around the Rhinogs, then north towards Trawsfynydd, curving around a geological structure known as the Harlech Dome. Although it is likely that the presence of gold here has been known since ancient times, it was not until the mid-1800s that the Welsh Gold Rush really started, the first 'official' discovery being reported in 1843. Over a period of about twenty years, a succession of mines were opened, yet while it is recorded that more than eighty mines had opened and had produced at least a small amount of gold by about 1860, most were derelict by 1870. Four mines proved the exception – Clogau, Gwynfynydd, Castell Carn Dochan, and Cefn Coch – and the continued success of these four mines resulted in a further and more intense gold rush in about 1887, after which there was a steady decline. Indeed, mining in the area had largely ceased by the time of the First World War. By the time of the Second World War, most of the mines were derelict and overgrown, many hidden beneath the encroaching undergrowth of the Coed y Brenin forest – the oldest and most extensive forest in Wales. Originally called the Vaughan Forest, it was renamed Coed y Brenin ('Forest of the King') in 1935 to celebrate King George V's Silver Jubilee.

In more recent times, both Clogau and Gwynfynydd Mines have been reopened sporadically to supply Welsh gold to the jewellery market, but at the time of writing, both are again closed. According to the recorded output of all the mines in the gold belt, a total of about 4 tons of gold has been produced to date, the lion's share being produced by Gwynfynydd and Clogau, with Cefn Coch and Castell Carn Dochan producing the vast majority of the rest. There is a continuing tradition that the wedding rings worn by the Royal Family should be made of pure Welsh Gold.

The walk starts from the car park (marked on OS maps) at the southern edge of Ganllwyd, where there are public toilets, an information board and a pleasant picnic area alongside the river. When leaving the car park, cross the main road and turn right along the pavement, follow this past the school and the houses, then recross the road to take the 'no through road' on the right, close to the 'end of speed limit' signs. Cross the bridge and bear round to the right, following signs to Tyddyn Gwladys, soon passing a small, fairly primitive building housing the local telephone exchange, with the sound of the rushing Mawddach river in your right ear. Follow the lane along the left side of the Mawddach gorge, soon entering a fine stand of trees – very tall, very old, and very nice! – where there are a profusion of ferns.

After about 600 metres you reach a car park at Pont Cae'n Coed, where there is an information board. There is also a footbridge crossing the Mawddach (across which you can, if you wish, later return), but your onward route continues along the surfaced lane, climbing gently all the time, with increasingly impressive views of the rushing river, and increasingly dense thickets of rhododendron – alluringly attractive, perhaps, but a choking and ecologically destructive menace nonetheless. After a further kilometre you pass (but do not cross) another footbridge, shortly after which you reach Tyddyn Gwladys (another car park), a short distance beyond which the public road ends and deteriorates to a rough track.

It is about now that you begin to see the legacy of the gold rush. Buttressed stone walls appear to your left, and the track you are following starts to reveal its antiquity – it must once have been an access route to the mines in the bottom of the gorge, to which it probably owes its origins. You soon pass Mostyn Cottage on your left, followed by the Ferndale Holiday Cottage complex on your right, developed from buildings that were once barracks for the miners. At Ferndale, keep to the left past the vehicle barrier (where there is the entrance to an adit), and follow the continuation of the track, soon reaching a short, steep climb beyond which there are more ruins on the left, the first of which

*Pistyll Cain.*

contains the remains of a waterwheel pit, with the brick-lined arches for the shaft and shaft end still very obvious to either side of the back wall. The further you go, the more intensive the ruins become, and it is not long before you sense and then see an impressive waterfall away to the right. This is Rhaeadr Mawddach, which you will get a much closer look at later, but for the moment, notice the large iron pipe to the left at the base of the falls – part of the water-supply system for the Gwynfynydd Mill.

The track soon levels, and more ruined buildings appear to the left. There are open shafts hereabouts, some of which are well hidden in the undergrowth and appear unexpectedly at ones feet, and some of the moss covered, crumbling masonry is very unstable, so if you are tempted to explore off the beaten track, I thoroughly recommend you do so with the utmost caution. Just beyond the confluence of the Afon Gain and the Afon Mawddach, the valley narrows, and the track swings

*The derelict Gwynfynydd Gold Mine. The modern settling tanks,*
*where the tailings were reprocessed, are to the right of the track.*

hard to the right and crosses an old, iron bridge. It is here that the
spectacular Pistyll Cain appears to the left – a particularly impressive
(and deafening) sight in high water conditions.

Having crossed the bridge, the track continues around to the right,
soon swinging left past a junction and climbing a shallow spur. Although
your onward route lies along the leftmost track, it is well worth taking
a short journey down the right track, which leads into the site of the
Gwynfynydd Mill, the buildings of which were totally destroyed by fire
in February 1935. There are several interesting remains here, and by
continuing until you are close to the river ahead, you get a superb view
of Rhaeadr Mawddach.

Back on the main route, the onward track soon passes the end of the
leat where water was taken from the river for the Gwynfynydd Mill,
shortly after which it reaches a beautiful old stone bridge. To the left, up
in the woods, there are levels and shafts, some with rotting ladders still

*in situ*, many treacherously hidden by encroaching undergrowth. While your onward journey lies across the bridge, you might like to take a short detour and continue along the track ahead for about 300 metres, to reach the lowest buildings of the Gwynfynydd Gold Mine, replete with modern warning signs. The two tracks to the left are inclines leading to the upper buildings and surface workings, but be aware that the mine does not lie on access land, so if you decide to explore, you should keep to the public rights of way.

Gold mining at Gwynfynydd dates from about 1863, by which time there were already several small gold mines in the area, the first find being made in about 1836 at nearby Beddcoeddwr. Although the Gwynfynydd mine was in existence before this time, it was mining mainly lead, but everything changed in 1887, when the Gwynfynydd miners found a very large pocket of gold. The discovery was initially kept secret because the Crown effectively owns all the gold and silver in the country, and mines finding these noble metals must pay a 'royalty', but the find at Gwynfynydd was so large that it was impossible to keep it secret for long, and soon Special Constables had to be brought in to guard the mine. Despite this rich find, and along with all the other mines in the area, there followed mixed fortunes, and the mine eventually closed in 1917.

Owing to increasing demand for Welsh gold for jewellery, mining at Gwynfynydd recommenced in 1981 and continued for several years. Such was the success of the new venture, that on 21 April 1986, the mine gave Her Majesty the Queen a kilogram of pure Welsh gold as a sixtieth birthday present – a Royal gift indeed! In the 1990s, the mine was taken over by Welsh Gold plc, and underground mining continued until 30 March 1999, after which time the emphasis changed to reprocessing material from the spoil heaps, a process that continued until a few years ago. The site currently lies largely derelict, and a strange sadness hangs over the valley.

Retrace your steps to the bridge (noting the older mine buildings on the far side of the river), cross it, and follow the track to the right, climbing steeply to a junction where you bear right, soon reaching an attractive, modern wooden seat where there are superb if wooded views of both falls and the site of the Gwynfynydd Mill. Continue to follow

RIGHT *The Mawddach Gorge just upstream of Ferndale. Note the tall masonry buttress on the extreme right of the picture – the remains of an unidentified mine building.*

BELOW *The Mawddach Gorge looking upstream from Pont Cae'n Coed.*

the wide track downstream for some distance, passing an adit entrance almost directly opposite the Ferndale Holiday Cottages, then trending right and slightly downhill at the next junction. Watch out for speeding mountain bikers on this section – Coed y Brenin is a popular venue and is renowned for the quality of its trails. There are waymarked routes here for all levels of experience, from straightforward rides to challenging trails with names like 'The Beast' and 'The Dragon's Back'.

Shortly after the junction, an obvious cutting to the right marks yet another mine entrance (now run in), and you soon come to a junction where a narrower path on the right leads across the Tyddyn Gwladys footbridge. Although you could cross this and retrace your steps back along the lane, it is more pleasant to continue straight ahead along the forest track, very soon reaching an outcrop of rock on the left with what appears to be bright turquoise paint streaked across it. There is a blocked adit here (look for the drill holes in the roof), and the bright colouration is not paint, but copper staining – formed by the weathering of a thin band of copper ore. More remains lie hidden in the surrounding undergrowth, and you get occasional glimpses of an older mine track through the undergrowth and trees to the left, most noticeably where it crosses small streams over well-constructed stone bridges and culverts.

Continue straight on along the track, soon reaching an obvious footbridge across the river where there is a plethora of waymarks. If you like, you can turn right across this bridge (signposted Yr Afon) and follow the path up to the lane, keeping left to retrace your steps past the telephone exchange, and thus back to the main road in Ganllwyd. However, by continuing on the forest track for just under a kilometre, you will come to yet another footbridge, which leads directly to the car park. This footbridge is on the right, just after the track descends to a meadow alongside the river, and a short distance past a stone building on the right. To access it, scramble briefly down a rough path to reach a gated, fenced corridor across the meadow. Having crossed the bridge, follow the path to the left and then zigzag up the bank past picnic tables to reach the car park.

You may have returned to your car, but this is not the end of the walk, for there is more fine and interesting walking to be had on the opposite side of the valley! So cross the road once again, then follow the pavement, this time to the left, as far as the obvious black, corrugated iron chapel. Turn right through the gate on the far side, and follow the lane which climbs steeply along the right bank of the stream – the Afon Gamlan – soon veering away from the water and entering ancient, mossy oak woods. About 300 metres along this lane, just before the second bend to the right, veer off slightly left to reach a post carrying a waymark (a green arrow with a white footprint on it), and follow a reasonable path leading back towards an increasingly noisy stream, where there is a footbridge. The roaring sound comes from the superb Rhaeadr Ddu, best viewed from a viewpoint reached by a reasonable path heading up and to the right, before the bridge. Curiously, there is a large slab here engraved with lines from a poem by Thomas Gray. I have been unable to find out anything about this stone, save that it is a replacement for the original very weathered engraving to its left, the origins of which seem lost in the mists of time. No doubt it has something to do with the nearby Dolmelynllyn estate.

*Rhaeadr Ddu – hidden among ancient oaks on the west side of the valley.*

*The settling tanks at Cefn Coch gold mine, with the ruins of the miners' barracks beyond.*

On the far side of the footbridge, various rocky paths lead to the top of the falls, which become more impressive as you climb. I leave you to choose your level of adventure on the basis that the closer you are to the river, the more difficult and slippery the path, but the more impressive the views. Just beyond the final, spectacular fall – a slot across the river – you reach another waymark pointing to the left, indicating a very narrow path through the woods. Follow this to reach an ancient, moss covered stone wall, then turn left alongside the wall following a faint, rocky path – not the easiest of routes in wet weather, for the rocks are really slippery. Despite the potential difficulties, this is a delightfully atmospheric place with an ancient feel, for virtually everything is covered in a thick layer of moss, and you could be forgiven for imagining that you are inside a fairy story. Indeed, these old, moist oak woods have survived as a relic of the original woodlands of this part of Wales, and are one of the richest sites in north-west Europe for liveworts and mosses. They are also home to a wide variety of woodland birds including the pied flycatcher, and if you come at the right time of year, you may even catch a glimpse of the increasingly rare brimstone butterfly.

You eventually reach a ladder stile and a rough, plank footbridge over a stream where there is another waymark. Ignore the waymark and the bridge, instead climbing the ladder stile and turning left on to an obvious (if wet) path through another delightful patch of deciduous woodland, eventually reaching the sadly inevitable conifers, soon after which you reach a surfaced lane. Cross this trending slightly left, to follow the continuation of the path on the far side, almost immediately passing another waymark pointing along the track, and soon reaching a recently rebuilt stone wall on the nearside of a stream. Follow the path along the right side of this wall, climbing steadily, soon emerging from the confines of the woodland into wonderful mountain scenery. Ahead lie the slopes of Y Garn, the south-eastern outlier of the Rhinogs, while slightly to the left, you begin to see the ruins of the Cefn Coch mine.

Ignore the modern forest track that brushes against your more ancient route from the right, continuing instead past another waymark on the original path alongside the wall, soon reaching a second waymark which points to the left, indicating a gap, closed off by an unusual stile, beyond which there is a weird wooden bridge. Pass the stile by pushing down (you'll understand what I mean when you get there), cross the strange bridge, then follow a series of stepping stones across the boggy ground beyond, climbing towards another waymark where you reach the Cefn Coch mine track. Turn left, and it is a simple matter to make your way up to the mine building from where there are spectacular views across the valleys of the Eden and the Mawddach, and on past Rhobell Fawr to the Arenigs.

Cefn Coch mine, a Site of Special Scientific Interest, was one of the richest gold mines in the area, although never in the same league as Gwynfynydd or Clogau. In operation between about 1862 and 1912, it is recorded as having produced some 1,392 ounces of gold. The site is quite complex and contains several interesting ruins, some of which have had remedial work done on them in an attempt to stop them deteriorating even further. The best way to explore here is to follow the track to below the large mill building, but instead of continuing to the miners' barracks (the furthest and most ruined building), walk up and to the right to the large mill building, passing the obvious remains of three, rectangular settling tanks. Having explored the mill – which would have been powered initially by water and (possibly) subsequently by steam – make your way up the hillside to the left of the building, and follow a good track – the mine tramway – that heads off to the left, below obviously disturbed ground where fences protect the unwary from unplanned descents of the stopes and shafts. The tramway is in

*The Cefn Coch tramway crossing one of the narrow causeways.*
*The small ruin to the right is that of the Powder House.*

a remarkably good state of preservation (you can even see the rails in places), and leads via two superb, narrow causeways to another, smaller building at the main adit entrance to the mine.

Turn back left and descend the obvious track (possibly an old incline) towards a small, square building (almost certainly the 'powder house' – where the explosives were stored), then make your way directly down to the stone wall below, and climb the oversized ladder stile to the left of the gate. Follow a waymarked path down through the bracken, making for another ladder stile at the bottom right-hand corner of the field. Climb this, and head just to the left of the ruined building, passing another waymark, to reach a stile to the left of the next gate. Go straight across the lane, and continue down the path to reach a footbridge. Cross this, go through the gate at the far side, and turn right on to an obvious path that descends through the oak woods, slowly getting further away from the wall to the right.

Towards the bottom of the hill and just before the end of the woodland, you reach a fence where there is a low fingerpost, easily overlooked. Go through the gate immediately ahead, and continue along the path until you reach a stone wall. Follow the wall to the left until it bends away to the right, then continue straight ahead until you can cross a stile across the fence on the right, a short distance ahead, heading towards farm buildings close to the road. You can see the gate leading to the road as you cross the field ahead, so make for a gap in the wall immediately to the left of the leftmost outbuilding, go through the gate, and turn left along the road to reach the start.

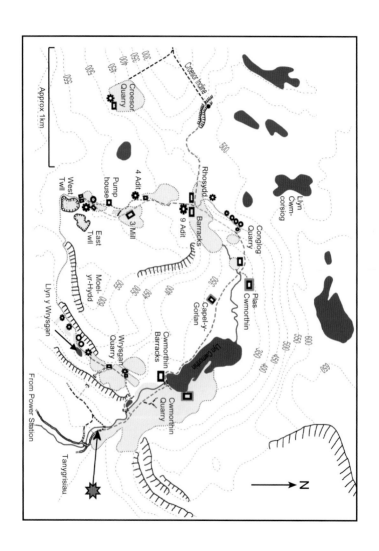

Croeson Incline

Approx 1km

000
450
400
350
500

Croeson Quarry

500

Llyn Cwm-corsiog

West Twll

4 Adit

Pump house

3 Mill

East Twll

9 Adit

Rhosydd Barracks

Conglog Quarry

Moel-yr-Hydd

500

600

400

450

Plas Cwmorthin

Capel-y-Gorlan

Llyn y Wrysgan

Wrysgan Quarry

Cwmorthin Barracks

Cwmorthin Quarry

Llyn Cwmorthin

350

400

450

500

550

600

650

From Power Station

Tanygrisiau

N

204

# 12.
# THE HONEYCOMBED MOELWYNS

A hidden gem which brings to life the breathtaking engineering of the slate miners of Ffestiniog. Even on a day when the summit of Snowdon is heaving with the excreta of the railway, you will find this area refreshingly quiet yet stunningly scenic, allowing you to experience a unique mix of Victorian melancholy and Ordovician exuberance. Prepare to be amazed.

## BACKGROUND INFORMATION

**Location** North-east of Tanygrisiau, near Blaenau Ffestiniog, in Snowdonia.

**Start & finish point** Rough car park at SH683454, at the end of a lane at the northern end of Tanygrisiau.

**Maps needed** OS Explorer OL17; Harvey Superwalker: Snowdonia: Snowdon and the Moelwynion.

**Map distance** 8 kilometres.

**Height gain** 300 metres.

**Terrain** The outward journey to the ruins of Rhosydd and the Croesor incline is all on good paths (except for the detours). From Rhosydd onwards, the route becomes progressively more difficult, with some dangerous ground above the workings, and potentially tricky route-finding during the descent.

**Duration** Allow 3 hours plus a fair amount of exploration time.

**Hazards** Unexpected drops, unpredictable subsidence, and difficult navigation in poor visibility.

**Public transport** There is a bus service to Tanygrisiau from Blaenau Ffestiniog, where there are two railway stations – one standard gauge, and one narrow gauge. The narrow gauge has a station at Tanygrisiau.

**Amenities/facilities** Blaenau Ffestiniog has all the facilities one would expect from a small town, including a Tourist Information Centre. The Llechwedd Slate Mine is open to the public and is a popular tourist venue.

GOD, THIS IS A DEPRESSING PLACE! Visit Blaenau Ffestiniog on a miserably grey day and you will find a miserably grey town, with great, brooding piles of spoil looming ominously through the mist.

Even the people seem grey, bent by the overbearing weight of their surroundings and its towering history. Everywhere you look there's slate and spoil, for this is the town that roofed the world.

The initial impression is one of total dereliction, of dilapidated industry and wanton environmental destruction. No wonder the Snowdonia National Park Authority don't want it. The fact that Blaenau Ffestiniog lies slap-bang in the centre of the National Park makes little difference – it is just too ugly to be included.

Or is it?

National Parks were originally created as a result of the National Parks and Access to the Countryside Act 1949, their two statutory purposes being firstly, to preserve and enhance the natural beauty of the area, and secondly, to promote the public enjoyment of the area. On this basis, I can understand why Blaenau Ffestiniog and its surroundings were excluded from the Snowdonia National Park, although I question the validity of some the reasons for its exclusion. However, following the Edwards Report in 1991, the Environment Act of 1995 altered the statutory purposes of National Parks. They are now, firstly, to conserve and enhance the natural beauty, wildlife and cultural heritage of their areas, and secondly, to promote opportunities for *public understanding and enjoyment of the special qualities* of their areas (my italics). As a result of this amendment, I believe that Blaenau Ffestiniog and its surroundings should no longer be excluded from the National Park because, as this walk will demonstrate, it has a strong cultural heritage and many special qualities, few of which are understood by the wider public. I also contest the view that the area is 'ugly' – but concede that beauty is in the eye of the beholder!

The walk starts unpromisingly from what, admittedly, is a scrappy little parking area above Tanygrisiau. The best approach from Blaenau Ffestiniog is to take the A496 towards Maentwrog. After just over 1 kilometre, turn right then immediately left following the signs to the Ffestiniog Power Station, pass a café on the right, then swing right and cross the narrow gauge railway via a level crossing. A short distance further, turn right across a bridge, then take the first turning left to reach the obvious, rough parking area beneath a towering spoil heap. You may well find the space crowded with outdoor centre minibuses – if there is no space for your vehicle, there is an alternative car park near the bridge you recently crossed, or you can park at the café (please ask for permission).

Unlike the slate quarries at Llanberis and Bethesda, both of which were predominantly surface workings, the Ffestiniog slate quarries are mostly hidden below the surface, and the spoil you see has been extracted from underground chambers. In fact, these slate workings are more mines than quarries, and the mountains here are riddled with passages leading to huge underground chambers. Some of the mines were fairly remote, so getting the slate to market was a major logistical problem, and the often innovative transport system has left many interesting remains. Indeed, the famous Ffestiniog to Porthmadog narrow gauge railway, one of the 'Great Little Trains of Wales', owes its very existence to the slate mines, for it was built primarily to transport the slate to the coast, from where it was shipped all over the world.

Before leaving the parking area up the rough track to the right of the waterfall, look along the line of cliffs to the left, where an obvious steep

*The amazing hanging spoil heaps of Wrysgan Quarry. The descent route follows the two upper inclines in the centre of the picture, then zigzags down spoil, grass and rock to reach the valley floor.*

incline appears to issue from the rock face. This is part of the transport system of Wrysgan Quarry, the surface remains of which you will visit during your return journey. Having identified the incline, leave the car park along the rough track, climbing steeply to start, with piles of spoil towering to your right. This waste material is from Cwmorthin Quarry, a vast complex of passages and galleries, parts of which are still worked on an occasional basis, which honeycomb the mountain to your right. Started in the early 1820s, the mine's heyday was in the 1860s when it became one of the largest in the area, producing huge amounts of slate. It eventually became linked with the gigantic Oakley Quarry, the entrance to which is on the far side of the mountain, and which claims to have been be the largest slate mine in the world. To give you some perspective, in the 1880s, this one mine had a workforce of just under 2,000 men, and produced around 60,000 tons of slate each year. There were twenty-six separate levels stretching a vertical distance of almost 500 metres, serviced by an narrow gauge railway with over 80 kilometres of underground track. One of the underground inclines was so wide that it accommodated six railway tracks running side by side along its entire

*Cwmorthin Barracks.*

length. What an incredible achievement . . . an amazing monument to human ingenuity and effort – even if it is mostly hidden underground.

The angle of the track soon eases, and the spoil of Wrysgan Quarry becomes increasingly obvious, coating the hillside to the left. Take note of this gravity-defying terrain, for you will descend through it on the return journey, rejoining your outward path via the bridge leading to the incongruous landscaped garden (more of which anon, at the end of this chapter). Continue straight on along the level track, ignoring the branch that veers off to the right, heading towards obvious ruins in the distance. You are now surrounded by claustrophobic spoil, the waste material generated by three generations of slate miners, but the view suddenly opens out as you reach the top of the rise and the unexpected waters of Llyn Cwmorthin appear, disappearing into the middle distance.

*The Conglog Tramroad through Cwmorthin, fenced with slate. The remains of Rhosydd Chapel sit forlornly by the Scots pines, while the equally ruinous Plas Cwmorthin hides in the clump of trees to the right. The Conglog spoil heap and incline are obvious, above and to the right of the chapel, as are the four open chambers of Conglog Quarry, above the Rhosydd track, which climbs the headwall from right to left. The lowest of the Rhosydd spoil heaps juts into the sky on the extreme left.*

The main entrance to Cwmorthin Quarry is further along the right side of the lake, but you should turn left across the old stone slab bridge and follow a good track along the left shore, passing below the enigmatic ruins of Cwmorthin Barracks, where the miners used to live from Monday to Saturday. Pass through a gate and continue along the track – the route of a tramroad linking Conglog Quarry (at the head of the valley) with the Cwmorthin transport network.

The views become more impressive as you meander around the lake shore, all the more so because of the dereliction you have so recently left behind. Cwmorthin is a magnificent valley that has managed to retain its beauty and atmosphere, despite it being scarred at both ends by slate quarrying. It is also predominantly treeless, because wood was such a valuable commodity, and the only trees that remain are around the Cwmorthin mine manager's house (where, strangely, there is a monkey puzzle tree – not exactly a native species), at Plas Cwmorthin (the Rhosydd Mine Manager's house), and at Capel-y-Gorlan (the Rhosydd Chapel). Slate, however, was available in abundance, and as you near the end of the lake, you will soon notice that all the fences in the area are made from slate.

Go through the gate and continue along the track, the remains of Conglog Quarry now obvious at the head of the valley, and with Plas Cwmorthin hiding in its grove of trees to the right, soon reaching Rhosydd Chapel, now in a very sorry state of disrepair. Built around 1867, this Calvinist chapel was used on weekdays as a school to educate the quarrymen's children, while on Sundays there was a Sunday school in the morning, and a meeting with a sermon in the afternoon. It was last used in the 1920s. When I first visited the area, well over thirty years ago, the building was still intact with a magnificent slate roof and a dry interior. Indeed, at that time it was still possible to identify some of the wall murals. Sadly, the roof slates were removed in the 1990s, effectively signing the building's death warrant, and hastening the deterioration that is all too obvious today.

The remains of Conglog Quarry become increasingly obvious as you continue along the track beyond the chapel, these including an incline running down the hillside below four shadowy holes. You will also see a track, curving from right to left up the Cwmorthin headwall before

*Rhosydd Chapel.*

disappearing behind a large spoil heap – the lowest of the Rhosydd tips.
Make a mental note of where the incline and track intersect, for it is here
that you will detour on your onward journey.

Conglog Quarry opened in 1876 and closed in 1909. It never had a
huge production, and was overshadowed by its immediate neighbours,
particularly Rhosydd. Indeed, the tramroad and many of its buildings owe
their very existence to Rhosydd. For example, the first building on the left
as you approach the site was the Rhosydd Stables, built for the packhorses
that used to travel the track between Rhosydd and the Ffestiniog Railway.
Moreover, the long terrace to the left of the gate at the start of the
headwall track was Rhosydd Terrace, built in 1865 to house the families
of Rhosydd quarrymen. The 1871 census shows that each of the tiny
terraced cottages was occupied by one quarryman, his wife, and between
one and three children. Luxury indeed! The tramroad immediately before
Conglog is in a particularly good state of preservation, and you can see
occasional rusting rails poking out from under the encroaching bog.

Before starting up the headwall track, you might like to visit
what is left of Plas Cwmorthin, the Rhosydd mine manager's house,

*Rhosydd Terrace. The pillars on the left once supported a wooden aqueduct, which carried water to power the mill, and the Conglog incline and spoil heap can be seen just beyond.*

approached along a good path from opposite the Rhosydd Stables. Built in 1860, this had four rooms on the ground floor (including a kitchen with a large range), one small and four large bedrooms upstairs, and a basement with a large stove. There was also a two-hole privy in the back garden. Like Rhosydd Chapel, it is now very dilapidated, yet still retains something of its atmosphere set, as it is, in a delightful grove. According to the 1861 census, it was occupied by the mine manager and his wife, together with four children, two servants, one visitor and two clerks. Ten years later this had altered to the mine manager and his wife, five children, one servant and a shepherd!

Leave Conglog through the gate and follow the rough track as it curves to the left up the head of Cwmorthin. Although you can follow this all the way to Rhosydd, there is a far more interesting route. Just beyond the point where the track intersects the Conglog incline, follow an indistinct path on the right that leads back to the top of the incline where there are several structures including the remains of the incline head, and the entrance to an adit. There is also a building with a deep, rectangular pit, but I have no idea what this was used for! Continue carefully across the very steep slopes ahead, trending up and to the left to reach a large hole – one of the original chambers sunk by the Conglog quarrymen. Turning so that the main track is below and to your left, traverse across the hillside, shortly to reach a second, larger chamber. The half bricked-up hole in its back wall is an early adit, probably driven to explore the area, eventually left inaccessible as the chamber was driven deeper in order to extract the slate. Take care in this area as the top edges of the chambers are vegetated and indistinct, and a slip could prove fatal.

Continue carefully in the same direction past two more, increasingly deep and impressive chambers, following the occasional remains of what must once have been a substantial path, eventually reaching the small entrance to a pedestrian adit, just beyond the fourth chamber. The onward path is indistinct, but just keep straight on, climbing slightly, heading towards the highest spoil heap you can see until, above and to the right, a small but obvious finger of spoil appears. Make directly for this, and as you climb, the views start to change, and you begin to get an impression of the place that once was Rhosydd.

From the tongue of spoil – the waste from Conglog Top Adit – follow a faint path towards the ruins of Rhosydd, heading for a fairly level grassy area on the near horizon, where there are excellent views of Rhosydd barracks and the incline leading to the upper levels. The stone wall here probably marks the boundary between Conglog and Rhosydd. To the right, the level, boggy area is all that remains of Llyn Coed, one of the water supply reservoirs for Rhosydd. Reservoirs such as this were extremely important, for water was the lifeblood of the mine, providing most of the motive power. Indeed, Rhosydd depended on water and used a huge amount, to the extent that even with twelve external reservoirs and two internal ones, the water sometimes ran short. During the hot summers of the 1870s, there were several complaints that the mine was forced to a standstill for lack of water. But it was not just summer droughts that caused a problem – during the prolonged frosts of winter, the whole system could freeze solid, creating the same problem.

*The view down Cwmorthin from the Conglog pedestrian adit, showing Conglog Mill, Rhosydd Terrace and Stables, Plas Cwmorthin, Rhosydd Chapel, the Conglog Tramroad, and the distant spoil from Cwmorthin Quarry.*

Walk across the remains of the dam (now forming the obvious stepping stones across the bog), and cross the stream at the far side where there are loads of bits of wood and iron, scant remnants of the water supply system. In addition to iron pipes, much use was made of wooden channels and leats, and you can just make out the course of one of these wooden troughs heading straight towards the obvious incline in the distance. Head towards the ruins to the left of the incline, meandering across rock outcrops in order to avoid the boggiest areas, and making your way down the right side of the shallow valley which carries the stream from Llyn Coed. You will soon see some masonry with large slabs of slate protruding from the left-hand side. Make your way to the top of this, then peer carefully over the edge to see a huge waterwheel pit, built during the final years of the mine but never actually used. Now negotiate loose slate to reach the top of the track from Conglog, and thus enter the melancholy Rhosydd.

Rhosydd Quarry was the biggest slate mine outside the main Ffestiniog group, with about 170 chambers arranged over fourteen floors. Started on a very small scale in the 1830s, the first serious attempt to extract slate came in 1852, but it took a long time to develop the quarry's full potential, and the mine was worked by a variety of companies over the years, most of which soon went into voluntary liquidation. Unusually for the time, this was very much a Welsh business, particularly after 1873, when the original Rhosydd Slate Company went into liquidation. In 1874, for example, 88 shares were owned by people living in England, against 264 by people living in Ffestiniog and Porthmadog. The Directors were always Welsh. Following a catalogue of disasters which began in about 1900, the mine finally closed in 1930, although caretakers kept the pumps going until 1948. Between 1949 and 1954, the walls of the mill buildings were systematically demolished and used to provide roofing slate!

The earliest record of Rhosydd slate being carried on the Ffestiniog Railway dates from 1854, although there is no evidence of Rhosydd slate being shipped out of Porthmadog until the following year. A major problem was the mine's remoteness and the consequent difficulty of transporting the slate to market. The earliest material was carried along a track built around the head of Cwm Stwlan, an arrangement that proved increasingly inadequate as the mine grew in size and the mills moved progressively down the mountain. In the mid-1850s, the then Rhosydd owners built a track down the Cwmorthin headwall and along the west side of Llyn Cwmorthin (the same track that you followed earlier), and until June 1864, slate was carried along this to Tanygrisiau. However, this was a controversial route because the land at the Tanygrisiau end was owned by the Cwmorthin Quarry company, who did not like a major competitor crossing their land. As a result, access disputes were common, and eventually locked barriers were built across the track, and huge tolls were sought. The mine was thus effectively suffocated, and the owners searched for ways around the problem, finally coming up with an ambitious solution in 1863. Their unlikely proposal was to build a new tramroad linking Rhosydd directly with Porthmadog via an awesome incline at the head of Cwm Croesor. Before continuing your exploration of Rhosydd, it is worth making a detour along the top part of this tramroad.

Ignoring the ruined buildings in front (you will explore these later), trend to the right and follow a faint but obvious path across the level terrace, getting a good impression of how extensive this place once was, eventually reaching a small embankment followed by a shallow cutting, at the end of which is a wooden gate. The low, slate building by the fence was the powder house, sited well away from the main settlement in case of accidental explosion. Once past the gate, the line of the tramroad becomes increasingly obvious as it curves around the right side of a boggy area, at times built up on a causeway, at others going through a shallow cutting. The spoil from Croesor Mine soon comes into view on the left side of the valley ahead, and just before the tramroad disappears around a bend to the right, low cairns to the left and right mark the junction with the miner's path to Cwm Croesor. A short way further, at the base of the embankment wall to the right, lie the rusting remains of a tram cart.

*Cwm Croesor from the incredible Rhosydd Tramroad, an engineering masterpiece of its time. The miners' path through Cwm Croesor climbs gently up the slopes to the left, crossing the Croesor Quarry incline, just beyond the spoil.*

Looking down the Croesor incline, with the tramroad snaking through the valley towards the distant Porthmadog. The junction with the incline from the Croesor Quarry is obvious at the bottom.

217

If the weather is fair and the visibility good, you will almost certainly want to stop as you round the next bend, for the views down Cwm Croesor open out dramatically, the tramroad becomes a narrow shelf carved into the headwall of Cwm Croesor, and it all starts to get very, very impressive. As you continue, ponder on the fact that the route you are following was built by pick axe, wheelbarrow, shovel and sheer brute force. What an amazing feat of engineering! What a bold way to solve the transport problems! But the most awesome part is yet to come. At the end of the shelf, just beyond a boggy section, you reach a low shelter with a large slab of rock hanging over the edge to its left. This marks the unlikely start of the Croesor incline, the winding gear of which is directly above your head.

Permission to build the Rhosydd Tramroad and Incline was granted by the owners of Cwm Croesor in 1863, and it was opened in late 1864. The incline is, without doubt, the most impressive in Britain, if not in Europe, falling a vertical distance of more than 200 metres over a horizontal distance of 380 metres, giving an average gradient of 1 in 1.86. However, this is not the full story, because the headwall (and thus the incline) is concave, making the top gradient far steeper – estimated at 46° or 1 in 0.97! The incline was operated entirely by gravity, the weight of the descending (laden) trams being sufficient to raise the ascending (unladen) trams, the speed of which were controlled by the 'inlineman'. His was a highly skilled job. Not only was the brake wheel (mounted on the large slab next to the shelter) highly inefficient, but the incline was effectively divided into three sections, so he had to know when to brake and when to release, almost to the split second. Despite this, accidents were surprisingly rare. The incline rails were finally lifted in 1948, at the same time as the Rhosydd pumps were turned off and the caretakers made redundant.

Having wondered at the incline and admired the stunning views down Cwm Croesor, retrace your steps to Rhosydd, noting the spoil and incline from Croesor Quarry, and the Miners' Track leading to Rhosydd, all on the left slopes of the valley. Rhosydd and Croesor Quarries shared a common boundary, and as each mine expanded, so the underground workings approached each other. Both accused each other of trespass, and in an attempt to settle the dispute by allowing more accurate surveying, it was agreed to dig a short tunnel to connect the two mines. As it happened, this proved that both mines had trespassed into the other's land, and once a settlement had been reached, it was decided to keep the tunnel open as an aid to ventilation, and as an emergency exit in case either mine suffered a serious accident. It was not long, however, before the Rhosydd manager had a small wall built across this passage, having discovered that workers from both mines were clocking in then leaving unnoticed through the other mine. The wall was designed in such a way that it still allowed ventilation and could be quickly brought down if the need arose. Nowadays, the wall has been partially demolished, and the aptly named 'Croesor-Rhosydd Through Trip', a serious and increasingly dangerous expedition, is regarded as one of the classic adventures for mine-explorers and underground enthusiasts.

Back at Rhosydd, continue to the far end, where an incline climbs up to the right, starting beside the entrance to a large adit out of which flows a sizeable stream. The twin terrace of buildings are the remains

*Rhosydd Barracks.*

of the Rhosydd Barracks. Because of its remoteness, many quarrymen lived on site during the working week. In 1865, there were more than 100 people living here, rising to about 150 in 1874, and it was only after about 1910 that the population began to reduce significantly. The buildings here – level 9 barracks – were built in stages, the southern terrace being built first, probably completed by 1866. The northern row (Barics Fawr) is believed to have been built sometime between 1888 and 1899, probably to replace earlier barracks, higher up the mountain. Not all the rooms were used for accommodation – there was also stabling, a changing and drying room, a fitting shop and various stores, the precise arrangements being largely dependent upon the number of employees. The 'street' between the terraces was actually the route of a tramroad taking spoil to the nearby tip.

Barrack life was not all sweetness and joy! For a start, the men had to pay rent of between 1½d and 3d per week. They also had to provide their own food and heating coal. They walked to the barracks each Monday morning carrying 'walats' (large white fabric bags) containing sufficient butter, eggs, bread, cake and bacon for the week. Living conditions at all the local mines were basic to the extreme, but Rhosydd Barracks, in particular, were notorious, leading, in 1887, to complaints from the local medical officer of health. He reported that the rooms were dirty and overcrowded, the shared wooden beds had lice-ridden straw mattresses, everything was damp, and there was little ventilation. To make matters worse, there were no latrines, the men using the spillway from 9 adit as a makeshift toilet. At the insistence of the medical officer, the barracks were improved – but not by much.

Living conditions may have been atrocious, but all sources agree that these barracks were the home, not of rowdiness and arguments, but of poetry, song and religion. The miners held debates, listened to visiting preachers, read the Bible, wrote poetry, and formed a 'mutual self-improvement class'. They also sang, and the Rhosydd Choir was renowned, winning the prize at the National Eisteddfod in 1898. It is said that on summer evenings the choir would process in full voice along the Rhosydd tramway to the top of the incline, and all the haymakers in Cwm Croesor would lean on their rakes to listen to the echoes rebounding from Moelwyn to Cnict.

*A retrospective view of the middle part of Rhosydd. Number 3 mill is obvious to the right, with number 4 barracks and the privy to the left in the middle distance. The peaks in the far distance are those of the Snowdon Horseshoe.*

Having explored, make your way to the base of the incline and the entrance to number 9 adit (meaning this entrance is 9 levels below the top workings), out of which usually blows a strong, cold breeze. Known as 'Y Lefel Fawr' (the Great Level), at just under 680 metres it is the longest in the Ffestiniog area. Started in 1862, it took eight years to drive and formed not only the main drainage level (hence the stream), but also the main transport route. It had an unusual railway system in that the track had three rails (the middle one being common to both the outward and inward tracks), with loops where wagons could pass each other. At the far end of the adit is 'Piccadilly Circus', a small chamber where several major passages meet, one of which is an internal incline which used to climb to daylight through the levels above, eventually emerging at the West Twll.

Underground working conditions were primitive, especially when compared to nearby Croesor Quarry, which led the industry in modernisation and innovation. Even in latter years, the Rhosydd miners worked by candlelight, electricity being a luxury found only in some of the main tunnels and a handful of machine rooms. Additionally, while most other quarries in the area had separate tunnels along which the men could reach the workface, here they shared the tunnels and inclines with heavily laden and inexorably moving tram carts. Despite this, the quarry had an excellent safety record, far better, for example, than Cwmorthin, which was known locally as 'Y Lladd-dy' (the Slaughterhouse)! However, this all needs to be taken in context, because the sobering fact is that between 1876 and 1885, the life expectancy of a Ffestiniog quarryman was just forty-four years.

Your onward journey lies up the nearby incline, best reached from the right after periods of heavy rain, when the stream issuing from number 9 adit can be knee deep. Look out for the remains of a small reservoir on the right a short way up. At the top, follow the path first to the left, then around to the right, and slowly climb the second, brutal incline! As you emerge at the top, directly in front of you lie the remains of level 4 barracks (the earliest barracks to be built, occupied from about 1859 to 1899), the obvious path in front heading right to reach a low, small building – the privy – a luxury missing from the more modern barracks below! Number 4 level is at the end of the cutting behind and to the left of the barracks.

Follow the faint path that leads to the left of the cutting, running parallel to a line of spoil on the left. What you are aiming to do is to climb to the top of this spoil, but at its right-hand end. You could walk along it if you so wished, but it is far more pleasant to walk on the grass, and you are not missing anything particularly interesting apart, perhaps, from the ruins of number 3 mill – the substantial ruins to the left. On reaching the top of the spoil, you will find the remains of a large reservoir (now drained) in front of you, with a dam along the nearest side. To the left, a further line of spoil heads into the distance and, again, you can follow this if you wish. However, it is more pleasant to follow the faint path along the right side of the drained reservoir, heading towards another small ruin – the remains of the pump house. Before you leave, however, glance back across the ground you have just covered, for on a good day, in the furthest distance, you will see the Snowdon Horseshoe.

From the pump house, follow a very faint path around to the left and up the shallow valley beyond, eventually making your way up on to the spoil to the left and heading towards the nearby ruins – the remains of number 2 mill. The obvious fenced area to the right protects a deep shaft used initially to remove spoil, and latterly to pump excess water from the mine. From here, follow the obvious path heading gently uphill to the right of another new fence, this one installed to prevent the unwary from entering an area of recent collapse. In basic terms, several chambers in the area of the mine below your feet are in a state of imminent collapse, and the movement has tracked all the way to the surface – as evidenced by the gorge-like cutting beyond the fence. The surface is still moving, and will inevitably continue to do so for some considerable time, so you would be well advised not to cross the fence! Instead, follow the path to its right – the line of one of the earliest inclines – climbing gently towards more ruins in the distance, and passing close to the entrance of number 2 adit (beyond the fence on the left), through which you can see daylight.

When you arrive at the top, the buildings on the right are one of the original smithies, while the buildings to the left are of unknown

*The breathtaking West Twll, dug by pickaxe and shovel! The scale here is simply monumental.*

purpose! These were the earliest buildings, dating from the early 1850s, and the pit beyond – the West Twll – is the oldest part of the quarry, disused since the 1860s. From this viewpoint you have no idea of the extent of this pit, so walk carefully along the track between the buildings, then turn right and follow a faint path around the right side of the pit, keeping well away from the edge for reasons which will soon become abundantly clear. The path soon curves to the left, and as you continue, so you start to get a better impression of the area. I have visited this spot countless times, but the view back across the pit never fails to fill me with a sense of awe. It is not just the depth of the excavation, it is the sheer size of the overwhelmingly huge passage that disappears into blackness. I find it humbling to think that it was dug entirely by hand. Over the past thirty or more years, I have brought many people to this spot – most have uttered sounds of incredulity, and none has failed to be impressed.

Continue around the edge of the Twll, soon spying the entrance to yet another huge passage at the base of the furthest wall, above which a small, level platform just below the lip marks the end of number 2 adit, through which you earlier saw daylight. You will also see various remains in the base of the Twll, including a huge double wheel, part of the machinery that once controlled the incline leading down to the end of number 9 adit. The close views may be awesome, but the longer views are equally impressive, the peaks of central Snowdonia forming a jagged horizon beyond the wilderness of Moelwynion. Continue around the edge of the pit, then break away to the right, following a faint path towards the right-hand cliff of Moel yr Hydd – the mountain directly in front – making for the lowest part of the shallow saddle on the near horizon, following the remains of what looks like a small leat. You will soon see the rear side of a sign, beyond which is a low, iron gate, through which you must eventually pass. If in doubt, or if the visibility is poor, keep trending right until you reach a wire fence, then follow this to the left to reach the gate. Do not touch the fence unless you want a shock – it is electrified!

While walking towards the gate, look to the right of the West Twll where there is a huge area of obviously disturbed ground – the East Twll. This is the site of the disastrous 'Great Fall' of 1900, when a huge area of the south-eastern part of the mine collapsed. Whether this was caused by the over-enthusiastic removal of some of the pillars that supported the roofs of the galleries (an easy way to get extra slate), or by geological problems, will probably never be known, but it had a dramatic effect on output, as it destroyed transport lines and effectively ruined what was then the most productive part of the mine. The business never fully recovered.

Go through the gate and follow a faint path down and to the left, below the summit cliffs of Moel yr Hydd, with panoramic views to the right, over the vale of Ffestiniog and on to Cader Idris, with the suggestion of Plynlimon beyond. Although not always obvious, this path is relatively easy to follow, leading down into the valley below cliffs streaked with quartz, and past large outcrops of pockmarked rock (all formed by the same metamorphism that created the slate), heading inexorably towards a small tongue of slate spoil at the base of a low

*The ill-defined descent route below the summit cliffs of Moel yr Hydd. You must ensure that you pass below the outcrop to the right of centre, heading for a small tongue of spoil, just visible on the right.*

band of cliffs marking the right edge of a narrow terrace. This is all well and good in reasonable visibility, but in misty conditions you must take great care to ensure that you have descended below the outcrops (see picture below). After a few minutes of descent, if you look back towards the saddle, you should be able to discern the line of the track built to take the earliest slate around the head of Cwm Stwlan. This eventually passed the Moelwyn Quarry, and then continued to the turnpike road at Llanfrothen.

Continue down the descent path, steep where it breaches the outcrops of the lower terrace, then very boggy for a short section, beyond which it rounds a corner and reaches a large rock by the tongue of spoil seen from the saddle. Regaining the path on the far side of this boggy section can prove awkward in misty conditions – the easiest option is to keep level and search for the spoil. The path passes behind the rock and over the top of an adit (the cause of the spoil) where there is a stone shelter,

then continues parallel to the line of outcrops. It is a strange path, varying in quality from a well-laid track to an indistinct rabbit run, but probably marks the line of a once well-trodden route used by miners from both Rhosydd and Wrysgan quarries. You soon reach a second area of spoil where the path is level with the adit entrance, then the path veers to the right to gain twin spoil causeways, the

*The cutting leading to the top of the Wrysgan Quarry main incline, the top part of which runs through a steeply descending tunnel.*

left one of which ends at adequate if meagre stepping stones, allowing you to negotiate another boggy section without too much of a problem. A short distance further, just over the rise, you will see the tiny, twin-dammed Llyn Wrysgan appear, nestled in among rock outcrops.

Although you can follow the main path directly to Llyn Wrysgan, by staying level to reach the top of the small outcrop ahead, you will come to another pile of spoil. Climb to the top of this where there is a flooded adit entrance, then turn right and continue carefully to the top of a pit very similar to those seen earlier at Conglog. This is part of the large Wrysgan Quarry, which was worked intermittently from 1851 to about 1946. Although never as large as Rhosydd, Wrysgan was a signifi-cant quarry in the area (as you will soon discover), with its own unique transport system leading directly to the Ffestiniog Railway. Continue to another large pit, almost directly above Llyn Wrysgan, with rusting ironworks in the rock slab at its lip, then head directly for the dam at the left side of the lake, carefully zigzagging down steep slopes to reach a line of spoil. Cross this and turn left down a grassy path – at which point you are back on the main route.

Leaving Llyn Wrysgan, the path curves to the left around a pile of spoil, and goes between a ruin and a wall to reach a much better path – the line of an old tramroad. Immediately to your left is the top entrance to Wrysgan Quarry, and a short visit is thoroughly recommended, as it will give you a good idea of what it must have been like to work in these mines! The passage leads directly into a small chamber open to the sky, often frequented by sheep seeking shelter, beyond which is a huge chamber which disappears into darkness, being lit only by a small skylight. Although the communication passage along which you have just walked continues for a considerable distance, and it is possible to descend the chamber to reach the lower levels of the mine, further exploration is to be discouraged, unless you are correctly equipped and know what you are doing . . . so retrace your steps to the entrance and continue straight on along the tramroad, which leads to the top of a steep, loose incline. Descend this, very carefully, to reach the wide, level terrace below – the main mill floor.

To the right, at the bottom of the incline, a very wet cutting marks the line of Wrysgan's unique transport system. Rather than risk wet feet,

*The surreal gardens at the bottom of the Wrysgan descent path.*

continue straight ahead on to the mill floor, then turn back right to reach the end of the wet section, at which point you can follow the track into a further cutting full of rusting winding gear. At the far end of this, a steeply descending tunnel has been cut through the rock, emerging into daylight at the top of the incline you saw earlier from the car park.

You can, if you wish, descend here to reach your car – a masochistic option and not recommended. Please note, however, that there is a hidden drop half way through the tunnel, down which you must climb, and that the surface of the incline is treacherously loose in places. On reaching the bottom, turn left along the lane, and follow this to a path leading past the waterfall to the car park.

It is easier (and more pleasant) to retrace your steps to the mill floor, then continue to the far end of all the buildings where you will see another incline. Gain this by any of several paths leading through the spoil, and follow it down to the next level. On reaching this, avoid the next incline by turning left in front of an old building, and continue to the end of the level, where an unlikely flight of stone steps lead down to yet another level. As you descend these, consider that the miners would have climbed up and down through these levels several times a day. Take care at the bottom as the steps are in a very poor state of repair, then look back and to the left to see the bottom entrance to the mine, out of which blows a cold, damp breeze. Now walk to the right to gain the bottom of the incline you just avoided, from where a good path descends into the valley, zigzagging to reach a much better track at the bottom, still following the line the miners would have taken each day on their way to and from work . . . six days a week, in all weathers, and without the benefit of modern fabrics! And as you gaze up and back at the spoil through which you have just descended, and forward to the spoil of Cwmorthin Quarry, I defy you to be unimpressed by the size of it all – by the mammoth effort that has taken place on and under these hills. No words or photographs can truly do the area justice – in order to appreciate fully, you must visit and explore.

At the better track, turn right and walk past the pool, through a gate, and into a surreal landscaped garden. Narrow paths encourage exploration, and hidden delights appear in the form of a Japanese bridge across a crystal clear pond full of grass carp, standing stones, domen, and a strange geometrical structure looking for all the world like some South American shrine. There are mining remains here too, rails and cogs and cutting gear, which give some clue to the garden's origin, for it was the retirement hobby of the late Robin Jones, a former slate worker. There is a strange calmness here – a weird tranquillity. It is a total enigma – it feels totally out of place – and yet there is a certain indescribable something about it. It is a work of art. When you have explored the garden, exit across the bridge on to the main path, turn right, and descend to the car.

It would be easy to romanticise this place and the work of the quarrymen – but the truth of the matter is that it was a cruel, gruelling life in squalid surroundings. But I do wonder if there were not times, when the weather was kind, that they stopped, and looked, and were amazed and overawed by the grandeur and majesty of it all.

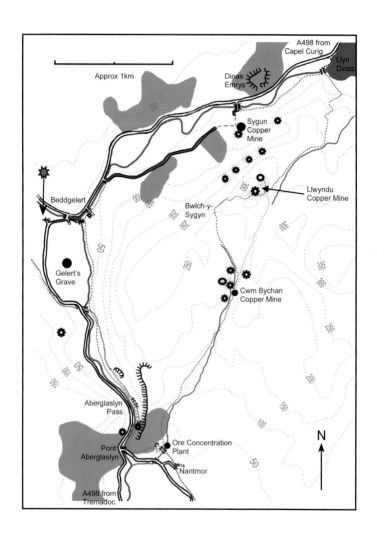

# 13.
# THE COPPER MOUNTAIN

A relatively straightforward hill walk on mostly excellent paths, offering spectacularly panoramic views for only a modicum of effort. Apart from the great scenery, the heritage interest is maintained throughout the journey, with heroic dogs, rushing torrents, forgotten railways, and a hill full of copper.

## BACKGROUND INFORMATION

**Location** The hills south-east of Beddgelert in Snowdonia.

**Start & finish point** Pay & display car park at SH588481, in Beddgelert.

**Maps needed** OS Explorer OL17; Harvey Superwalker – Snowdonia: Snowdon and the Moelwynion.

**Map distance** 10 kilometres.

**Height gain** 260 metres.

**Terrain** Excellent paths for the most part, with a short section along a quiet country lane. The descent to Llyn Dinas, however, is not kind on the knees.

**Duration** Allow 3 hours plus exploration time.

**Hazards** Open shafts and loose rock around the mines. The section between Cwm Bychan mine and Bwlch-y-Sygyn can be very muddy after wet weather, but the worst is avoidable. Although relatively gentle, the section around Bwlch-y-Sygyn can be awkward in poor visibility, and standard mountain safety precautions apply.

**Public transport** Beddgelert is served by several bus services, and by the Welsh Highland Railway between Caernarfon and Porthmadog. The nearest main line railway stations are at Porthmadog, Caernarfon, and Betws y Coed.

**Amenities/facilities** Beddgelert is a busy tourist destination with all the usual gift shops, pubs, hotels and guest houses, and a highly recommended, award winning ice cream parlour. There is a general store and a post office, but no bank. There are public toilets by the footbridge in the village, and at the National Trust car park at the bottom of Cwm Bychan.

WAY BACK AT THE START of the thirteenth century, there lived in the fastness of Snowdonia, an ambitious prince named Llywelyn. In 1205, he made a shrewd political choice and married Joan, the illegitimate daughter of King John of England. Thirteen years later, in the Treaty of Worcester, the English Crown recognised him as the ruler of all Wales. So much for the facts.

Legend has it that King John gave Llywelyn an Irish Wolfhound named Gelert. So strong and fearless was Gelert that he soon became Llywelyn's favourite hunting dog, always accompanying the prince and his wife when they went out hunting. It was their custom on these occasions to leave their baby son in the care of a nurse and a servant. Unfortunately, the nurse and servant did not take their duties too seriously, and sometimes left the baby unprotected while they pursued other pleasures.

One fateful day, several hours into the hunt, Llywelyn noticed that Gelert was missing. Puzzled and more than a little displeased, he called off the hunt and headed home. As the party dismounted, Gelert came running out of the castle, covered in blood and wagging his tail, whereupon Llywelyn rushed inside to the nursery to find the cradle overturned, bloodstained bedclothes all over the floor, and no sign of his son. There could only be one conclusion. Filled with grief and anger, he drew his sword and, with one great stroke, he slew the dog. But Gelert's dying whimpers were answered by the sound of a baby crying from behind the overturned cradle. With a mixture of relief and horror, Llywelyn snatched aside the cradle to find his son, totally unharmed, with the bloody body of a huge wolf next to him. It was now obvious that Gelert had killed the wolf as it tried to attack the baby. Filled with remorse, Llywelyn buried Gelert in a nearby meadow, and marked his grave with a cairn of stones. It is said that he never smiled again.

The story of Llywelyn and Gelert is one of the best-known folk tales of Snowdonia . . . yet it is a complete fabrication, invented in the early nineteenth century by the manager of the newly built Beddgelert Hotel (now the Royal Goat Hotel) and several other local men, as a means of encouraging tourism to the area. While the name Beddgelert can be translated as Gelert's Grave, it is actually a mutation of Bedd Celert (Celert's Grave), the Celert in question being the leader of a community of monks who established a hermitage in the area in about AD 700. By 1230, around the time when Llywelyn is supposed to have killed Gelert, the hermitage had grown into an Augustinian Priory with a stone-built church – now the Beddgelert parish church. Nevertheless, the ploy worked, and Beddgelert is today a bustling tourist village, and each year, thousands of people visit what they are led to believe is Gelert's grave.

The car park is easy to find, the signed entrance being close to the Royal Goat Hotel on the A498 at the Tremadog end of the village. Leave the car park and head left into the village, passing an excellent Tourist Information Centre *en route*. Resist the temptation to visit the wonderful ice cream parlour (save this for later), and continue along the street, turning right immediately before the bridge and walking alongside the river, past craft shops on the right, to a narrow footbridge at the confluence of the rivers Glaslyn and Colwyn. If, like me, you like to escape the worst of the crowds, cross the bridge and turn right on to a concrete footpath that heads downstream, eventually reaching the Welsh Highland Railway where it crosses the Glaslyn river at the start of the Aberglaslyn Pass. Alternatively, if you wish to visit Gelert's Grave, turn right just before the footbridge and follow the signs to the grave, then continue downstream on a good path to reach the railway, where you cross the footbridge to reach the same point.

*Heading towards the Aberglaslyn Pass alongside the Welsh Highland Railway.*

The Welsh Highland Railway Company, founded in 1922, comprised an amalgamation of several earlier railways including the Porthmadog, Beddgelert and South Snowdon Railway, and sections of the North Wales Narrow Gauge Railways. These railways were mostly built to carry slate, so the timing of this new company was none too good . . . the slate industry was just about to nose dive into a steep decline. The company lasted just five years, going into receivership in 1927, and the railway was finally closed in 1937, the rails being lifted not long afterwards. Determined efforts to revive the railway started in the early 1960s, but nothing physical happened until 1997. The revived Welsh Highland Railway now runs from Caernarfon to Porthmadog, where it joins the Ffestiniog Railway, thus creating a new 65-kilometre 'Great Railway Journey'.

Using the official, signed route, cross the railway with care, and immediately turn left on to a good path alongside the railway, heading downstream towards the Aberglaslyn Pass, the scenery becoming more and more impressive with each step. Eventually, the path leads you close to the rushing torrent, and the section through the narrowest part of the gorge is an exhilarating and noisy experience when the river is in spate, but please note that sections can become impassable when the water levels are exceptionally high. Immediately before the first wooden walkway, look over your left shoulder to see the entrance to a trial adit – a short, dead-end passage hewn by miners in search of copper. If you have a torch, this adit can be followed to its end with little problem apart from the potential for wet feet.

Shortly after the wooden walkways, the path climbs away from the river through woodland, soon arriving at Pont Aberglaslyn, a delightful, ancient stone bridge. Do not go through the gate on to the road, but turn left and climb the obvious rocky steps to reach a more level path with a broken wire fence to the right, the roar of the river receding, fading into a stillness full of woodland birdsong. Follow the path through the woods, trending left above a cottage to reach a gated gap in a stone wall, then continue to where a signed a path leads back and to the right, winding down to reach a National Trust car park, where there are toilets and an interesting information board through a gate on the right.

Continue through the obvious arch under the railway embankment, beyond which is a pleasant meadow where there are some odd-looking structures ahead and to the right. These are the remains of a small ore

*The path through the Aberglaslyn Pass, recently refurbished owing to the reopening of the Welsh Highland Railway.*

concentration plant, built in the early 1920s to serve the mines further up the valley. Most prominent are two circular concrete depressions known as buddle pits. Fed with water from the nearby stream, and probably powered by a small waterwheel which turned brushes within the circles, these buddle pits used gravity to separate valuable minerals from the lighter rock dust in crushed ore, the heavier minerals settling near the centre of the buddle from where they could be removed. There are also several concrete bases (possibly the remains of a crushing plant), and a strange circular iron cage with a pulley at the top, possibly some form of tensioning device associated with an aerial ropeway that ran between here and the mine, although its precise purpose is unknown.

Your onward route follows the obvious path that leads up and into the woods on the left of the valley, soon merging with a wider, steeper track which shortly becomes narrow and rocky before emerging from the trees. A short distance further and you pass through a wooden gate, following the well-defined path up an increasingly beautiful valley in a series of steps, sometimes steep and rocky, sometimes more level, passing the scant

*Cwm Bychan. Walking here is a total contrast to the recent journey through the gorge.*

remains of some of the pylons that carried the aerial ropeway, and pausing occasionally to catch your breath and gaze back at the widening views and the distant shimmer of Cardigan Bay. The path eventually crosses the stream, passes to the right of some ancient sheepfolds, and then levels out near the remains of some mine workings. There is a ruined building with a stone bench, a low entrance to a flooded adit, and a line of aerial ropeway pylons continuing up the valley. These remains are all associated with the Cwm Bychan Copper Mine (also known as the Nantmor Mine), the main part of which lies opposite a strange looking, horizontal wheel that marks the end of the aerial ropeway, only a short distance further on.

Little is known about this mine, and what there is tends to be confusing and contradictory. The first workings in the area are believed to date from the early eighteenth century, the heyday of copper mining in this area being between about 1782 and 1802. Almost a century later, in 1870, the Cwm Buchan (*sic*) Silver Lead Mining Company was registered in London, but little is known about its circumstances apart from the fact

*Cwm Bychan Copper Mine. The main spoil heap is obvious to the left of the aerial ropeway pylons. The onward route curves to the left along a side valley, immediately in front of the patch of light rock – a quartz slab.*

that work on the northern, lead-rich lode had ceased within five years. The last period of activity occurred in the early 1920s when the Nantmor Copper Company Ltd was formed. It appears that the main activity of this company was all above ground, with the construction of the aerial ropeway and the concentration plant down by the railway, but – for reasons that are unclear – little if any ore actually passed along the ropeway, and the company went into voluntary liquidation four years later.

Apart from the aerial ropeway, the most interesting part of the mine lies above the large, orange spoil heap, at the top of which is the entrance to an adit, used not only to drain the mine, but also to bring ore to the surface. It is possible to find specimens of both iron and copper pyrites here – some may look like gold, but don't get too excited! To either side of the adit, narrow, indistinct paths leads up the hillside to a flatter area where there is more spoil, the remains of a powder-house, and the entrance to the stope – the deep, narrow chasm formed when the ore was extracted. Although fenced around its top, this is easy to enter through the obvious

*The open stopes at the top of Cwm Bychan Copper Mine. Great care is needed here, as the drops are considerable!*

cutting, and is an impressive sight that is well worth a visit. However, be aware that the drops are considerable and care is needed.

Having explored, descend to the end of the aerial ropeway and continue up the valley, which soon forks. Here, hidden behind a rock step and a small pile of spoil to the right, is another adit, most likely the one driven to explore the lead rich northern lode. Straight ahead, the start of the eventual descent route is just to the left at the end of the narrowing valley, but this direct route only shortens the journey by a few hundred metres, and misses out some of the most interesting and scenic parts of the walk. It is therefore better to trend left up the side valley, soon passing the entrances to two more adits, side by side, probably driven in an attempt to find a continuation of the copper lode. Keep to the right side of this valley to avoid the worst of the bog, climb a short, steep step, then continue more easily across a flatter area towards Bwlch-y-Sygyn – the shallow, V-shaped groove on the horizon straight ahead. Pass to the right of a couple of ruined shelters where another grassy path comes in from the left, then follow the steepening path, rocky with reddish coloured stones, which leads directly to the top.

The change of scene is as breathtaking as it is sudden. The ground levels, then falls away at your feet, dropping almost 300 metres to the flat valley floor, the southern slopes of Craig Wen forming a wild backdrop.

*The view from Bwlch-y-Sygyn – as spectacular as it is sudden. Yr Aran dominates the skyline, with Snowdon behind, and Lliwedd to the right, directly below which is the rounded, partially wooded dome of Dinas Emrys.*

To the left, the brooding bulk of Moel Hebog dominates the scene, with the northern end of the Nantlle Ridge, a shape-filled skyline beyond. Slightly right, and almost directly below, the rocky prominence of Dinas Emrys squats solidly in the valley, above which the slopes rise to the wilderness of Yr Aran, and on towards the summit ridge of Lliwedd. On a clear day, it is easy to imagine that you can see the people clinging to the summit pyramid of Snowdon. After the recent confines of the valley, it is an almost agoraphobic vantage point, and a grand place to stop for some refreshment. At the right time of year (May/June), when the rhododendrons are in flower, the hillside below is purple, and the air is sweet with scent. But here is a paradox, for the rhododendron, although undoubtedly attractive when in flower, is nothing short of a rampant weed which is smothering the hillside and destroying the native flora. Originally an escape from the nearby Craflwyn estate, the National Trust is making great efforts to prevent further encroachment (and, indeed, to reduce it) both here, and in the Aberglaslyn Gorge.

Having supped and stared, follow the path around to the right, traversing steep slopes, past the scant ruins of a mine building, to a finger-post, then continue straight ahead and follow the path as it swings to the right through a short, shallow valley to reach a rocky bowl full of dead bushes – the result of efforts to kill the rampant rhododendrons. The path swings hard left then curves to the right as it climbs across the blighted back wall of the bowl, finally emerging at a wire fence. Turn left to reach a ladder stile, cross it, and continue to the wasteland that once was the Llwyndu Copper Mine.

Also known as the Grib Ddu Mine, the Llwyndu Copper Mine had a promising start. Although, like so many mines in this area, the

details are sketchy, it is believed that the mine opened in the late 1830s, the extracted ore being dressed (crushed) on site by twenty girls: 'the cheapest thing we have on the mine and without them it is hardly possible to know what we should do'. By 1841, the mine was approaching 40 metres deep, and a vertical shaft was dug to the east of the site so that water and ore could be raised more easily using a large, horse-

*Llwyndu Copper Mine. The remains of the paved cobbing floor are obvious in the foreground.*

powered windlass known as a whim. This also meant that the ore could be dressed lower down the hill, probably much to the relief of the girls, who would have had to work in the open in all weathers. However, all was not well, for regular floods were making it difficult for the ore wagons to ford Llyn Dinas, and the quality of the material in the lode was deteriorating. By 1842 the mine was in financial trouble, and by 1845 it was up for sale. Although there are no further details, it is assumed that there were no buyers and that the mine was abandoned soon thereafter.

Despite the passage of time, the mine has survived remarkably well, and several interesting features are still visible. The first is the cobbing floor, the paved area to the right of the path, where the girls would have dressed the ore by hand. To the right and above the paved area, are the remains of a stone building, probably built so the girls had some shelter in particularly inclement weather, 'to keep them as comfortable and happy

*Llyn Dinas from the start of the steepest part of the descent.*
*Lliwedd is the obvious high peak to the left.*

as possible as I assure you they are quite essential to our success'. To the left, partially filled and hidden behind some boulders, is the adit entrance, above which are two obvious holes, both of which lead immediately to the top of the stope – an impressive vantage point that requires care should you choose to climb the loose slopes for a visit. Beyond the cobbing floor, up to the left, and just before the finger post, are the scant remains of a stone flue running up the hillside. These are the remains of a lambreth, where carefully selected, crushed ore was roasted in a crudely built chamber, the resulting fumes travelling along the flue, depositing minerals (mainly arsenic), which were removed periodically.

At the finger post, the descent route continues straight ahead, but it is worth making a short detour to the left, following an old causeway towards the lower ore dressing area – obvious with its mounds and platforms of tailings. By walking to the left behind the first wall, then climbing a short step, you arrive at the site of the horse whim, the large boulder that acted as a bearing for the windlass still in place. Turning left and climbing another short step, you quickly reach the top of the shaft – now covered with a metal grille. Below this area are the walls of several ruined buildings, the purpose of which is open to conjecture, but all of which must have been associated either with dressing the ore, or with providing shelter.

Back at the finger post; follow the loose, rocky track leading down into the valley, steeply and awkwardly at first, then more gently, with stunning views over Mynydd Llyndy and the wilds of central Snowdonia. Eventually, the waters of Llyn Dinas swim into view, and the path steepens again as it zigzags painfully down to the shore, following a route built by the miners to allow horses to travel between the mine and the valley. At the lakeside, turn left through an awkward kissing gate, and ignoring the footbridge, continue straight ahead along a fair path leading downstream with the river to your right. The ditch to your left is all that remains of a leat supplying water to the Sygun Copper mine ahead – more of which anon.

In front, but on the opposite side of the valley, is the rocky prominence of Dinas Emrys, an important site not only in Welsh and Arthurian folklore, but also in British history. It is reputed to be one of the locations of the Holy Grail, it is central to the story of the Red Dragon of Wales, and historians believe it to be the place where King Vortigern retreated from the Saxon hoards and his disgruntled countrymen.

According to the *Mabinogion* – that wonderful book of eleven (sometimes twelve) fantastical tales that lie at the heart of Welsh folklore – Dinas Emrys was the place where Llud Llaw Ereint, the Celtic god of Health and Healing, imprisoned two fighting dragons – one white, the other red – beneath a pool of mead. If you want to know more details, you will have to read the *Mabinogion* – a pleasurable task that is thoroughly recommended. Centuries later, King Vortigern retreated here and ordered his men to build a tower. Each day, they would start to build the walls, but each morning when they returned, they would find the masonry had collapsed. Vortigern was advised that the only way to stop this happening was to sprinkle the blood of a fatherless boy (an orphan boy, born of the fairies) over the walls. Accordingly, he searched the country for such a lad, and eventually found him in Carmarthen. The boy's name was Myrddin Emrys (the Welsh name for Carmarthen is Caer Myrddin – Myrddin's Castle), and over the years, Myrddin has been Anglicised to Merlin! Keen to prevent any blood being spilt (particularly his), Merlin persuaded Vortigern that the problem was the two dragons imprisoned beneath the hill. These were then uncovered, whereupon they fought a fierce battle, the Red Dragon of the Britains finally killing the White Dragon of the Saxons. So impressed was Vortigern with Merlin's prophecy, that he gave him the site when he moved on towards the Lleyn Peninsula (see Walk 15).

Interestingly, archaeological excavations done in the 1950s revealed that the site was occupied by the late Roman period, but that most of the earthworks are of later origin. The poorly built stone banks had been rebuilt several times, and there was evidence of iron working and several buildings clustered around a central pool. Shards of Middle Eastern amphorae and Phoenician red slip dishes dating from the fifth century (the time of Vortigern) suggest that the site was occupied at that time by an important chieftain, rich enough to import wine. The footings of the tower and central cyst are later, dating from the late twelfth century – about the time of Prince Llywelyn (the one with the dog).

A short way past the far end of Dinas Emrys, you reach the Sygun Copper Mine, which is well worth a visit if you have the time or inclination, although the bouncy castle and archery range do not sit comfortably with its mining heritage. Dating from the 1830s, this Victorian copper mine had a very checkered history, but is an important industrial archaeology site, not

*The River Glaslyn leaving Llyn Dinas at the bottom of the descent route.*

least because it is the location of one of the first oil flotation plants in the world. Invented by Frank and Stanley Elmore in 1896, and patented in 1898, the Elmore Flotation Process allowed increased amounts of valuable copper to be extracted from poorer ores, and is still used (in a more advanced form) to this day, throughout the world. The Elmores took over the Sygun Mine in 1897, and set about building a mill to house their flotation process. This proved extremely costly, and the mine, although technologically advanced, was a commercial disaster, mainly due to over-optimistic forecasts of the quality of the available copper ore, combined with plunging copper prices. The mine finally closed in 1903, and the site fell into dereliction – apart from being converted, briefly, in 1958, into a Chinese town for the Ingrid Bergman film *The Inn of the Sixth Happiness.*

In 1986, Sygun was renovated and reopened as a tourist attraction, and two years later, the Amies family, who spearheaded the renovation and without whose determination the attraction would not exist, were awarded the Prince of Wales Award for 'the sensitive development of visitor facilities at Sygun Copper Mine', and for providing 'an excellent and informative experience of the underground world of the Victorian miner'. The underground trip is an experience not to be missed.

*Approaching Sygun Mine – the square tower-like structure on the horizon. The curse of the rhododendrons is all too obvious here.*

Leave the mine along the narrow lane which heads west along the valley floor, starting immediately below the small waterwheel below the buildings, and passing to the right of a field full of lumps (and often rabbits!), soon reaching a gate (usually open). Follow the lane past a curiously out-of-place grove of eucalyptus trees, a caravan, a ruin and several cottages, and continue to a bridge where the lane joins the main road. Do not cross the bridge, but climb the ladder stile on the left and follow the riverside path downstream to reach another bridge on the right, which you should also ignore. Instead, follow the alley straight ahead to reach Beddgelert village green and the footbridge at the confluence of the two rivers.

Retrace your steps to the car park, not forgetting to pay a well-earned visit to the ice cream parlour *en route*!

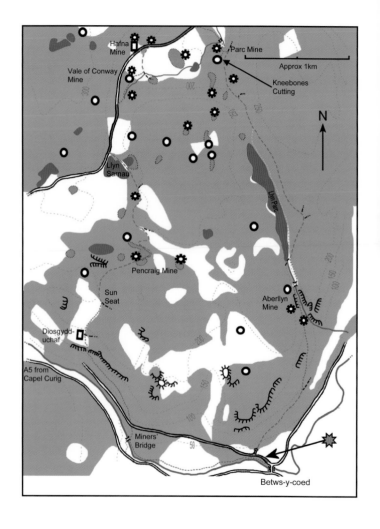

Approx 1km

N

Hafna Mine

Parc Mine

Kneebones Cutting

Vale of Conway Mine

Llyn Sarnau

Llyn Parc

Pencraig Mine

Sun Seat

Aberllyn Mine

Diosgydd-uchaf

A5 from Capel Curig

Miners' Bridge

Betws-y-coed

# 14.
# HIDDEN HOLES & LOST LAKES

A fascinating walk, mostly on good paths and tracks, exploring a world camouflaged by conifers above the Conway Valley. Despite (or, perhaps, because of) the forestry, the often unexpected views are stunningly expansive, and even in the depths of the forest, the surroundings are seldom without interest.

## BACKGROUND INFORMATION

**Location** The Gwydyr Forest, to the north of Betws-y-Coed in Snowdonia.

**Start & finish point** Pont-y-pair car park (SH791568) in Betws-y-Coed. This pay & display car park fills early in the high season – other car parks exist, and there is (free) roadside parking on the main road at the western end of the village.

**Maps needed** OS Explorer OL17; Harvey Superwalker – Snowdonia: Glyderau and the Carneddau.

**Map distance** 12 kilometres.

**Height gain** 400 metres.

**Terrain** Reasonable paths and good forest tracks for the most part, with a couple of short sections on quiet lanes.

**Duration** Allow 4 hours plus exploring time.

**Hazards** Old mine workings are extremely dangerous for the unwary. There are many deep shafts and workings in the area, some of which are surprisingly well concealed by the undergrowth, so it would be prudent not to wander away from the beaten track. The start of the descent route from Diosgydd-uchaf through the forest is very steep and can be especially tricky after wet weather, and the riverside path downstream from the Miners Bridge is impassable if the river is high. Beware, also, of speeding mountain bikers on the forest tracks!

**Public transport** Betws-y-Coed is served by several bus routes and has a railway station.

**Amenities/facilities** Betws-y-Coed has all the facilities you would expect from a thriving tourist village, including a bank and post office, an excellent tourist information centre, a great Spar store catering for walkers, several gear shops, and a wide selection of gift shops, hotels, guest houses, restaurants and bars. There are public toilets in the car parks at Pont y Pair and the railway station.

BETWS-Y-COED IS A POPULAR, BUSTLING VILLAGE lying snug in a deep, steep-sided valley, the surrounding hillsides cloaked with densely planted conifers. But it has not always been this way. A little over 400 years ago, the area was clothed predominantly in deciduous woodland, the trees thinning as they climbed towards high, heather moorland where the frequent rock outcrops had been scratched and pockmarked since Bronze Age times by people worrying the landscape in their search for copper, zinc and lead. It was a quiet, tranquil area, and hardly anything had altered during the preceding millennium, but things were about to change. In 1607, Sir John Wynn of Gwydyr, a significant figure in Welsh history, began mining for metal with a hitherto unseen intensity, and so began a theme that would continue well into the twentieth century.

The coming of the Industrial Revolution in the mid-eighteenth

century had a huge affect on the landscape here, as in many other places. Between 1850 and 1919, lead and zinc mines dominated the area; the wild uplands and wooded valleys became full of noise and smoke, and the scars and waste from the mines fast became a major landscape feature. Then, inevitably, came the decline. As the world price of lead and zinc tumbled, so the mines became uneconomic and were

*The gated entrance to number 4 adit, Aberllyn Mine.*

slowly abandoned, their remains left to rot and recede into the landscape. The last to close was Parc Mine, which managed to keep going until as recently as 1963.

The most recent radical landscape change began in 1921, when the then Forestry Commission planted the huge Gwydyr Forest, effectively obliterating the hard industrial landscape beneath an equally hard blanket of conifers comprising mainly sitka spruce, Norway spruce, Douglas fir, Japanese larch, Scots pine, and tsuga (hemlock). In total, over 7,000 hectares were planted, just under 5,000 of which are still productive woodland with a felling rotation of between twenty and forty years. Following a growing and welcome trend throughout Wales, felled conifers are not automatically replaced with more conifers – instead, many areas are now being replanted with native hardwood species such as ash, beech, and sessile oak, thus providing a wider range of habitats and changing seasonal colour.

Despite first appearances, the forest is not totally without character or interest, for hidden within the serried ranks of conifers are some of Wales's most important upland oak woods. Parts of the forest have been designated as Sites of Special Scientific Interest, and particularly important are the lichens, one of which survives in its largest concentration in North Wales over an area of almost 30 hectares. There are many fine stands of timber over eighty-five years old, and some of the Douglas firs and Norway spruces have been around for almost two centuries, predating the most recent afforestation by many years. Additionally, the legacy of the mining has added another dimension to the landscape, and there are extensive surface remains including old mills, engine houses, waste tips, shafts, adits, and reservoirs. Much of the ore was processed locally, and large waterwheels were originally used to provide the necessary power. Although none of the actual wheels survives, the wheelpits in which they turned still remain and are a common feature. In recent years, some of the more important sites have been partially restored, and several now have excellent interpretive displays.

Parking in Betws y Coed can be a nightmare, particularly during holiday periods (or, increasingly, on sunny weekends at almost any time of the year). Although there is free roadside parking along the main A5 road at the western (Capel Curig) end of the village, the most convenient car park for this walk is along the lane to the left at the far side of the ancient, stone-built Pont-y-Pair (the Bridge of the Cauldron), which carries the B5016 over the Afon Llugwy. Built in 1468, the bridge is a great vantage point from where to watch salmon leaping up the cascades. It is also a popular launch pad for those who feel the need to jump into the river. Locals call the eastern parapet (above a deep pool), the 'silly side', and the western parapet (above sharp rocks), the 'suicide'.

From the car park, walk uphill along the lane that leads away from the bridge, and take the first turning to the right. Continue past the houses, veer right where the road swings round to the left, and follow the green waymark towards Llyn Parc along a gently rising forest track. Immediately beyond the brow of the hill, bear left up an obvious but narrower, rougher path, and climb more steeply through the trees, crossing some very steep ground with big cliffs above you to the left, and occasional, tantalising glimpses of expansive views to the right. Go straight on at the junction, and continue to climb steadily, the path soon curving left along the side of the picturesque Aberllyn gorge.

At the top of a particularly steep, rocky section, a small stream crosses the path from left to right, issuing from a low, partially collapsed mine entrance. This is part of the Aberllyn mine, which was worked for zinc on six levels between about 1869 and 1906, and was thus one of the last mines in the area to close. The larger, gated entrance to the number 4 level, out of which issues a strong, cold draught, is only a short distance away, at the far end of the terrace of spoil to the right. Within the forest, all the shafts and entrances close to paths have been capped or gated in an attempt to prevent the casual visitor from entering what is an exceptionally dangerous environment, but this has been done in such a way that the bats that roost in the mines are still able to enter and exit without hindrance.

Continue up the main path, soon passing the entrance to Aberllyn number 3 level on the left, before reaching the top of the gorge. Here there are yet more remains, including an obvious capped shaft high up to the left, and a large, stone-built retaining wall with yet another gated entrance at its left end. Follow the path below the wall and round to the left, past a small waterfall and across a footbridge, and continue along a much better path to reach Llyn Parc, a narrow, sinuous, isolated reservoir which once supplied water to the Parc Mine mills. Bear right along a wide forest track.

A short way along this track, a path with a yellow waymark heads off to the left and descends towards the shore of the tranquil lake. Although this is, without doubt, the prettiest route, the path is rough and awkward at times, and is often overgrown. With this in mind, you may prefer to continue along the main forest track, bearing left at the first junction, the far end of the lakeside path joining from the left just after the brow of a hill. Continue along the main track to a Y-junction, where you take the leftmost track and start to descend quite steeply, with glimpses of the distant Hafna Mine with its obvious, iconic chimney, across the valley to the left. Follow the track straight down the hill until it becomes a tarmac lane, shortly after which you reach an obvious path leading off to the left. Head down this path towards the wide, surfaced terrace, but almost immediately cross a stile on the left to reach Kneebone's Cutting – an impressive open stope from where lead ore was mined. The deep stope contains a couple of abandoned mine trucks, various wooden props and stemples, and the entrances to several passages, and there is often a strong, cold draught blowing from the depths – particularly noticeable (and pleasant!) on hot summer days. There is also an excellent information board here detailing the various jobs done by the miners.

*The sinuous Llyn Parc – once the water supply for Parc Lead Mine.*

*LEFT* Kneebone's Cutting, looking almost vertically down. Note the wooden stemple (top right), and the gated adit (just above and left of centre). A chill, sulphurous draught often issues from this gash.

*BELOW* The extensive ruins of the Hafna Mine mill – a well preserved site with excellent informative displays. Note the iconic chimney at the top left of the site.

Retrace your steps to the stile, and make your way to the far side of the flat, surfaced terrace where there is another interpretive board, this one telling you about Parc Mine, the last mine in the area to close. Although commercial mining actually finished in 1958, Parc mine reopened again briefly in the early 1960s as part of a research project into new milling techniques. Little now remains of the extensive spoil heaps and buildings (the area having been 'landscaped'), but the streams to either side of the level platform both issue from the mine, as is evident from the reddish colour of the stream bed (caused by iron staining). It is difficult for us to comprehend what life was like for these miners in the late nineteenth and early twentieth centuries. Certainly, there was huge hardship, but with this came great camaraderie. Many of the miners were members of the Llanrwst Male Voice Choir, and the hills often rang to their music as they walked home at the end of their shift.

Leave the level terrace at the opposite side to Kneebone's Cutting, and follow an obvious if sometimes narrow path across the stream and into pleasant woodlands. Continue to a lane and turn left, climbing steadily for about 500 metres to reach Hafna Mine, where there is a forestry car park. Hafna Mine was in operation from about 1879 until the early part of 1910s, and there are some exceptionally well-preserved buildings here, including a smelter and chimney. There are also several very informative interpretive boards, and the site is well worth a visit. Perhaps the most interesting approach is to climb to the top (where you will find the main adit and shaft entrances at the back of a level, grassy terrace), and then descend, level by level, exploring each in turn with the help of the information boards.

Having completed your exploration, return to the road, turn left and retrace your steps down the hill for a short distance, turning right almost opposite the Hafna car park sign on to a wide, forest track, which curves to the right below the mine. This track soon bends round to the left, and at the head of the bend, you should turn right along a less well-defined but obvious footpath (waymarked as part of the Iron Trail, but with the waymarks facing away from you!). Go past some wooden steps on the right, which lead to ruined mine buildings, and continue past a capped shaft to some substantial ruins – the Vale of

*The Vale of Conway Mine, showing the capped shaft and remains of the mill building.*

Conway Mine mill building – where there are fine examples of both a waterwheel pit and a buddle pit (where the ground ore was separated from rock debris). There is an excellent interpretive display board to the left, beyond the buddle pit.

Perhaps the main reason that these ruins are in such a good condition (relatively speaking) is that this mine is a classic example of over-enthusiastic marketing. Despite extravagant claims about its potential, and like the vast majority of the mines in this area, the Vale of Conway Mine was never very profitable. Indeed, within twelve months of its opening in 1876, the only employee was a caretaker! The lovingly built waterwheel and buddle pits saw little use, and were thus still in excellent condition when the mine closed.

Continue along the footpath on the far side of the mine, following what must have been an important miners' track, with fading reminders of the past wherever you look. There are just so many remains up here – a slowly disappearing testament to a way of life that has all but faded from popular consciousness. The path soon enters a tiny but delightful valley where there are wooden steps, more entrances, and then a small but babbling brook, before it bends sharply to the right and ends at a lane – the same lane, in fact, that you followed earlier to reach Hafna Mine. Ignoring the direction shown by the Miners Trail waymark, turn left and follow the lane to the top of the hill, past a couple of houses, an old chapel, and the entrance to the Nant Bwlch yr Haearn outdoor pursuits centre, soon reaching Llyn Sarnau, where you turn left on to a good track between the outdoor centre and the lake.

Follow the track as it bends to the right and crosses the (often dry) lake on a causeway, the ground to the left composed largely of tailings from the nearby Llanrwst Mine (you may have noticed its chimney on the hillside above the outdoor pursuits centre). Continue straight on through the woods on the far side of the lake, soon reaching a junction

*The view across Llyn Sarnau towards Moel Siabod.*

where you go straight ahead, past a vehicle barrier, and on along the track with a sloping grassy field to your left. Where the track curves to the left, the vista to the right opens out dramatically, and you get excellent views across to Moel Siabod. Soon afterwards, the track starts to descend and curves to the left again, at which point you should veer down a track to the right, curving right then winding down the hillside in a wide zigzag, soon passing the spoil from yet another mine (probably Pencraig Mine), below and to the right. The track then swings around to the right and passes the remains of a stone building, also to the right. This was almost certainly the Pencraig Mine mill – the evidence for this being not only the presence of a waterwheel pit, but also the extensive spoil heaps to the left of the track, which are composed of fine crushed material known as tailings.

Beyond the mine, the track plunges into dense forestry. Ignoring obvious tracks to the left and right, keep straight ahead along the main track until, after a slight ascent, the woods to the right come to an end at a grassy field, and the views open out once more. Turn right over a ladder stile (the 'sun seat' signposted to the left is simply a bench in a sunny position!), cross a second stile a short distance away, and then follow the obvious path down the left edge of the field, sandwiched between an ancient wall to the right and a more modern forest fence to the left, following the route taken by the miners who used to walk to work from Betws-y-Coed each day. If the first part of this path is muddy (as it often is), avoid it by detouring on to the field to the right. You soon reach another stile, beyond which the path continues between the wall and the fence, descending to the left of a ruin to reach a farm track near an isolated house known as Diosgydd-uchaf. Go straight across the track and follow a continuation of the path to the left of the wall, crossing a rough field and turning left through a hole in the wall (look out for blue-topped wayposts), and then head for the obvious ladder stile at the edge of the forest. The path beyond this stile starts very steep, very rocky, and potentially very slippery – so take your time!

Once at the bottom of the steep section, take note of your surroundings. You are now in dense woodland, descending steeply along a continuation of the path used each day by the miners to get them from Betws-y-Coed to their workplace and back. The further you descend, the better and more pleasant the path becomes – a well-worn shelf across some very steep ground – and the more ancient and impressive become the surrounding trees. You can almost imagine the miners walking up and down this track every day (except Sunday), probably singing on their way back from work, but maybe not on their way there! There is even a friendly footbridge across a small stream – a modern replacement for the original stone bridge, the only remains of which are the masonry buttresses to either side. Admittedly, the tranquillity is spoilt somewhat by the noise of the traffic on the A5, hidden on the other side of the valley, but once the first, steep section has been overcome, it is still an easy and very pleasant descent.

Continue straight ahead at the first track junction, entering an area of exceptionally fine, tall firs, before merging with a tarmac lane. You can, if you wish, bear slightly left and follow the lane all the way back to Pont y Pair car park – a good option if the river is high. It is more interesting, however, to cross the lane and continue the descent along the same line, following a rough and sometimes steep continuation of the miners track to reach the famous Miners' Bridge across the Afon Llugwy – a popular tourist attraction. The easiest but least scenic onward route is to cross the bridge, climb the bank on the far side, and then turn left alongside the road, following the pavement all the way to Betws-y-Coed. Alternatively, it is more pleasant (if not so easy) to turn left on the nearside of the bridge, and follow the rough, bouldery, and flood-prone path downstream, alongside the river.

Eventually, you reach a ladder stile, beyond which is a pleasant field. Follow the path across the field and over a modern footbridge, continue to a second, older footbridge made of stone slabs, then climb the ladder stile and enter a well-trodden area of woodland where there are picnic tables and an excellent boardwalk that meanders and splits around the trees, and which enables the wheelchair-bound to enjoy something of the beauty of the area, away from the main crowds. Continue downstream, either on the riverside path or on the boardwalk, soon returning to the Pont-y-Pair car park and so-called civilisation. The contrast is bleak, for on sunny summer weekends, you can smell the fish and chips, and it is difficult to ignore the mindless shouts of drunken yobs as they cavort on the rocks above the bridge.

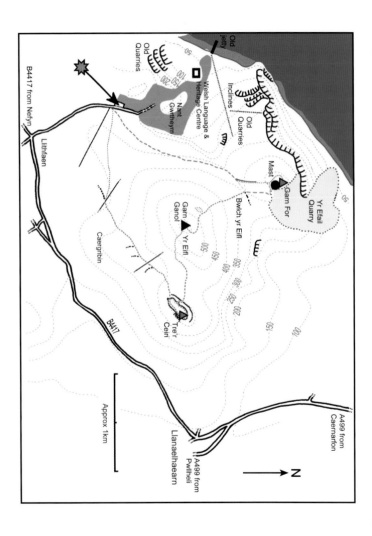

Old jetty

Old Quarries

Old Inclines

Old Quarries

Nant Gwrtheyrn

Welsh Language & Heritage Centre

B4417 from Nefyn

Llithfaen

Caergribin

B4417

Garn Ganol

Yr Eifl

Bwlch yr Eifl

Mast

Garn Fôr

Yr Eifl Quarry

Tre'r Ceiri

Llanaelhaearn

A499 from Pwllheli

A499 from Caernarfon

Approx 1km

→ N

# 15.
# IN SEARCH OF THE ANCIENTS

A not-so-gentle walk to one of the most impressive Iron Age sites in Britain, taking in the highest peaks of the Lleyn Peninsula, with stunning views in almost every direction. Although not particularly high, the mountains have a surprisingly serious feel, due in no small measure to the nature of the terrain.

## BACKGROUND INFORMATION

**Location** The northern coast of the Lleyn Peninsula.

**Start & finish point** Large car park at SH353440, at the head of Nant Gwrtheyrn (Vortigern's Vale), signposted from the village of Llithfaen, on the B4417 between Llanaelhaearn and Nefyn.

**Maps needed** OS Explorer 254.

**Map distance** 7 kilometres.

**Height gain** 400 metres.

**Terrain** Good tracks and paths to start and finish, but steep, narrow, loose and intermittent rocky paths on the way up and down the three summits.

**Duration** Allow 3 hours, plus an extra hour or so to explore Tre'r Ceiri.

**Hazards** Scree and loose boulders on the three summits, with potentially tricky route finding in misty conditions.

**Public transport** An infrequent bus service runs through Llithfaen, and there is an hourly bus between Caernarfon and Pwllheli. The nearest railway station is at Pwllheli.

**Amenities/facilities** There is a pub and a shop in Llithfaen, and an excellent information centre and licensed café at the Welsh Language Centre.

SHORTLY AFTER I BOUGHT my first car, many summers ago, I drove to Stonehenge on a murky day, and walked through the mist to that most iconic of ancient monuments. This was in the days before the new road was built, before the noise of traffic stole away the silence, and before the madding crowds made it necessary to restrict intimate inspection. Standing within the inner circle next to the altar stone, the rest of the world hidden behind a curtain of mist, the atmosphere was tangible, almost oppressive. Time weighed heavily. This was a rare moment, one that has lived with me, and nowhere else have I experienced such a powerful feeling . . . except at Tre'r Ceiri – Town of the Giants.

Tre'r Ceiri is spectacular. No other description does it justice. Lying at over 450 metres above sea level, at the top of a steep, rocky hill, and occupying an area of some 2.5 hectares, it is nothing less than an ancient town protected by a largely intact wall. In addition to two narrow, well-defended main gateways, there are three 'posterns' (built to allow townsfolk to collect water from nearby springs), and the most well-preserved sections of wall still have a parapet walkway with ramps and steps leading up from the inside. There is also an outer defensive wall with just one gate, protecting the most vulnerable, north-western approach. Dating from about 100 BC, it is believed that Tre'r Ceiri was once home to about 500 people, and within the encircling wall, parts of which are more than 3.5 metres high, lie the substantial remains of about 150 well-built hut circles, grouped together in four or five clusters. These huts vary in shape (from rectangular to circular) and in diameter (from about 3 metres to about 8 metres), and several are amazingly well preserved, with carefully built stone walls of over a metre in height. It is supposed that each hut would originally have had a conical roof of heather or turf, supported by a central wooden pole. An important archaeological site, the evidence unearthed here suggests that the original Iron Age town was strengthened and reoccupied during the latter part of the Roman occupation, and all of the significant finds here have been dated between AD 150 and 400. Having said this, a number of sources suggest that the site was largely abandoned by the end of the fourth century.

The whole of the landscape here has an ancient feel to it, and the area is crowded with legends. This is nowhere more true than in the valley of Nant Gwrtheyrn – Vortigern's Vale – above which the walk begins. Local tradition has it that this narrow, sheltered, almost hidden valley is the place to which King Vortigern fled after having betrayed the Britons by allowing the Saxons to gain a foothold – the same King Vortigern who had previously retreated to Dinas Emrys, as described earlier in Walk 13. The old OS maps of the area used to show a site called Castell Gwrtheyrn (Vortigern's Castle), and although the precise location of this was never specified, and is now long lost, several people have speculated that Tre'r Ceiri might have been the spot. Certainly the age is right, as is the time that it was abandoned, but the history of Vortigern – like that of Arthur – is now so cloaked with legend that it is doubtful that the truth will ever be known. Some stories tell that he was killed by Ambrosius, arguably the rightful King of the Britons; others that his 'castle' was struck by 'fire from God' (lightning?) and that he and his entire family perished in the fire.

Whether Vortigern used the valley or not will probably never be know for sure, but what is certain is that fishermen eventually settled in the valley. Until comparatively recently, it was a remote place with extremely difficult access, and as time went by, more and more stories were born. For example, tradition has it that the valley was cursed three times by three monks who received less than a warm welcome when they sought shelter there while on a pilgrimage to Bardsey Island. One monk foretold that the valley would never be holy so that no one could be buried there; the second monk said that the valley would enjoy success three times, but that each success would be followed by failure, and that the final failure would last for all eternity; the third monk stated that no two people from the same family would ever marry.

By the eighteenth century there were three farms in the valley, Ty Hen, Ty Canol and Ty Uchaf, but it was still an isolated place with difficult access, and life was hard for the tenant farmers. Despite the increased habitation, the stories kept coming. From this period comes the tale of Elis Bach, a dwarf who lived in Ty Canol, and whose legs were only 30 centimetres long, but who used to move with remarkable speed and agility over the rocky terrain. His job was to gather the sheep and goats ready for market, but he was never seen on the day itself. There are also stories about him defeating sheep robbers. A fanciful story, perhaps, yet local records show that an Elis Bach, from Ty Canol, died at the age of fifty-five in about 1849, ten years before the valley was changed forever by the coming of the quarries.

The valley is also the setting for one of the saddest and most poignant of Welsh love stories. Rhys and Meinir were childhood sweethearts who lived on neighbouring farms in the valley, their favourite meeting place being an ancient hollow oak on the slopes of Yr Eifl. Love blossomed, and they were eventually betrothed. At the time, a strong local tradition was that of the 'Wedding Quest', whereby the bride would hide on the morning of the ceremony, and the groom would have to find her. So on the wedding day, immediately after breakfast, Meinir slipped away from the valley and headed for the hills. A short time later, Rhys and his friends began the search, but could find no trace of her. By noon, the men assumed that she had eluded them, so they made their way to the church expecting that Meinir would be waiting, but she was nowhere to be seen. Hours passed, and Rhys became frantic with worry, eventually running all the way back to the valley where the search continued by torchlight until the early hours. But she could still not be found. The search continued for weeks, but no sign of Meinir could be found, and so the search parties became fewer and smaller until, eventually, only Rhys was left, still frantically searching every day. Stories soon began to be told of a madman who searched for his lost love among the wilderness of the valley slopes.

Thirty years went by, and still Rhys searched, frequently going to the ancient oak where they had met so many times. And then, on one stormy night, as Rhys was making his way towards the tree, the oak was struck by lightning and split in two. There, trapped within the hollow

*Yr Eifl (The Rivals) from Nant Gwrtheyrn car park.*

heart of the tree, was a bleached, white skeleton, still wearing a wedding dress. It is said that, as he cradled her remains, he died of a broken heart, and was found two days later with the corpse still in his arms. They were eventually buried together in the same grave.

To this day, there are common reports of ghosts in the valley – two ghosts, moving hand in hand – one, a man with a long white beard, the other, a woman wearing white. The ancient oak still stands above the modern village, and it is said that no bird will perch on it except for the owl (associated in Celtic myth with the god of oak trees) and the cormorant (associated with the god of the sea and storms).

The peace of the valley was shattered in the latter half of the nineteenth century with the arrival of the quarrymen, and quarrying continued here until comparatively recently. Indeed, a jetty was built so that the stone could be transported by sea, and the village of Porth y Nant was built specifically to house the quarrymen. According to the 1886 census, there were at that time over 200 people living in the 'Nant', as it had become known, over three quarters of whom were Welsh speaking. There was a chapel but no school, and the children were 'educated' by the minister in his house. There was also no inn, and once the quarrymen had become bored of rolling beer barrels down the hill, they began to visit the tavern in nearby Llithfaen. However, after a few ales, the journey back to the village down the steep sided valley was fraught with peril, and there are many stories of accidents, and even deaths.

By the time of the First World War, the main quarry in the valley had closed, and although quarrying did restart in a small way during the inter-war years, it quickly stopped after part of the village was destroyed by a landslide in 1925. There now being no employment here apart from subsistence farming, what remained of the village was virtually in ruins by the end of the Second World War. Although there were a few squatters for a while, the valley had been totally abandoned by 1959. But that was not the end, for in 1978 the village was bought from the then owners, and work began to turn it into a Welsh Language Centre – a role that continues, increasingly successfully, to this day.

Now you know the history of the area, it is time to explore it on foot. To get to the start of the walk, take the narrow lane that heads north from the crossroads in Llithfaen, and continue to the top of the hill, just beyond which you will come to a large car park on the left, sheltered by a conifer plantation. The access road to the Nant Gwrtheyrn Welsh Language and Heritage Centre is straight ahead, and the centre is definitely worth a visit if you have time at the end of your walk. In addition to a highly informative heritage centre and an excellent licensed café, Caffi Meinir, the surrounding area is fascinating, and there are extensive remains of the former quarry workings. Accommodation is also available in self-catering holiday cottages.

Back at the top of the valley, turn right out of the car park, and after only a very short distance, at a finger post, turn left on to a wide, rough track, heading towards the obvious saddle between the two peaks ahead. The views down into Nant Gwrtheyrn and across the former quarries on its north-eastern slopes get better, almost with every step,

as do the views along the north Lleyn coast towards Porth Dinllaen and Morfa Nefyn.

Some people argue that the views from the right-hand peak, Garn For, are the best on the Lleyn Peninsula (I happen to think that those from Garn Ganol are better), but either way, a trip to the summit is something of an adventure – although it has to be said that the ascent is something of a detour away from

*Nant Gwrtheyrn and the northern Lleyn coast from Bwlch yr Eifl.*

the main route, and can easily be avoided. If you do wish to climb it, continue along the track until it begins to level out at the saddle, where an ancient stone wall strikes off to the left, heading towards the very obvious communications mast, which whistles loudly in windy weather. Follow this wall to its far end, then carefully make your way over loose rocks to the summit, keeping to the left of the mast and its enclosure. Have gazed your fill, retrace your steps to the mast compound, then head downhill to pass between two small stone buildings and gain a grassy track leading down to the saddle. The onward path up Garn Ganol, the main peak of Yr Eifl, is directly in front.

To reach this path without climbing Garn For, simply continue along the main track to the top of the saddle, just beyond which a gate on the left gives access to a grassy track leading up towards the mast. The onward path is to the right, immediately opposite this gate.

It has to be said that the path up Garn Ganol, while obvious to start with, is not the easiest of routes – and it gets harder the higher you climb. The slopes are relentless, but the unfolding views easily repay the effort, and it is not as bad as it looks, as long as you take it steadily. There is little to break the ascent, apart from the rocky remains of an ancient quarry, off to the right about half way up, after which the path becomes steeper and slightly more difficult to follow as it meanders through the heather, whin and boulders. Take your time on this section and stop if you want to admire the views. When moving, keep focussed on the path, as the vegetation can easily hide ankle-wrenching holes between the boulders, and particularly in misty conditions, the route-finding here can be tricky. Although less than 600 metres high, this is a mountain in every sense of the word, and it has a serious feel to it, far more so than many of its higher but more rounded cousins elsewhere. Eventually the angle eases, and the path curves slightly right and heads directly towards the rocky summit with its stone-built trig point. On blustery days, there is a welcome shelter near by, where you can escape the wind – not that it helps much when it is raining! However, in all but the worst conditions, many people will forego the shelter in order to gaze in wonder, for it is from the summit that you get your first views of Tre'r Ceiri, sitting atop its rocky peak with the Glaslyn Estuary as a backdrop.

*Tre'r Ceiri from Garn Ganol.*

If you were unhappy with the path up Garn Ganol, you will hate the path down the other side. But first, you must find it. Starting from immediately below the trig point, head roughly south on an intermittent path – little better than a narrow sheep track – that meanders through the boulders. Ignoring paths heading off to the right, keep trending left along this often muddy path as it descends towards the flat ground in front of Tre'r Ceiri, taking care on the rocky sections. Although sinuous and far from the best, the path is fairly obvious once you are on it, and it is decidedly preferable to a more direct, cross-country approach, as the terrain is very difficult and it would be easy to turn an ankle, or worse. The flat land of the saddle, when you reach it, is little better – boggy at the best of times, it is a quagmire after wet weather. Sticking to the path seems to be the best option (all the detours I have tried have resulted in wet feet), and whatever else you do, keep going, because if you stop, you will sink! Luckily, this section is only short, and once you reach the heather on the far side, you are home and (hopefully) dry.

Once you have gained the relative simplicity of the heather, just head directly towards Tre'r Ceiri, which just keeps on getting more and more awesome the closer you get. I defy anyone not to be impressed. The path, now obvious, leads directly to the only gateway through the outer defensive wall, where there is an excellent information board describing the history of the settlement, as far as is known. Beyond this outer gate, the path curves to the right, and then climbs up to the huge main wall, the inner rampart, which it passes by means of a narrow, well-defended passage.

Immediately you pass through the gate, the hut circles become obvious. These are far more solid and substantial than many people expect, looking more like the remains of circular, stone built cottages than 2,000-year-old huts. And it doesn't stop there, for the more you explore, the more spectacular the place becomes. You can easily spend a delightful hour exploring, and it is definitely worth keeping an eye on your watch, for time seems to have little meaning here.

*Garn Ganol (left) and Garn For from within the walls of Tre'r Ceiri.*

Although the choice of route is largely yours, and I would encourage you to explore at your own pace and inclination, perhaps the best route on a first visit is to turn left beyond the gate, and follow the inner wall in a clockwise direction. As you climb towards the highest point of the hill, you almost immediately come to a group of hut circles, beyond which you pass one of the three, narrow postern gates that pierce the main wall like tall windows. The summit is only a short way beyond, and not only is it a spectacular viewpoint, but it is also the site of a substantial Bronze Age burial cairn, which must have been a central feature within the settlement. It does appear as if this cairn was carefully preserved by the people who built Tre'r Ceiri, and one must therefore conjecture that they viewed it with a certain degree of respect.

On clear, sunny days, the views from the cairn are stunning in almost every direction. In more sombre, misty conditions, there is a palpable antiquity, and the sound of the wind in the stones is like the murmur of a thousand voices, lending the area an evocative atmosphere that, while

*The view north-east from the highest point of Tre'r Ceiri.*
*The Menai Strait shines in the sunlight, top left.*

heavy, is never sinister. The feeling I get here, however, is different to the one I experienced at Stonehenge. That was one of pure, unadulterated power – this is one of mellow antiquity. There are ripe pickings here for a fertile imagination!

Continue to follow the wall in a clockwise direction, now heading gently downhill, passing some sizeable rock outcrops which form part of the defences, getting excellent views of the south-western half of the settlement. There are huts of all sizes and shapes all over the place, some with their stone walls and entrances virtually intact, others in a ruinous state. At the lowest point of the walls you reach the main gate, which faces south-west. Go through this, and carefully descend the (often slippery) rocky path to reach a wooden barrier where there is another excellent information board, then turn right along the reasonably well-defined path that descends into the valley. Alternatively, you can complete the tour of the walls to end up at the gateway through which you originally entered, retrace your steps to the outer gate, then follow

*The onward route from the south-western gate of Tre'r Ceiri. The path crosses the wall by the white patch in the centre of the picture, then goes through the centre of the shallow saddle beyond.*

*The onward route from the kissing gate on the Lleyn Coastal path. The path traverses the hillside, then heads towards the car park through the shallow saddle just left of centre.*

an indistinct path to the left to reach the same point. Whichever route you choose, what you need to do is reach the gap in the stone wall which crosses the flat land in the shallow saddle ahead. This is best achieved by following the path until you reach a section composed of laid stone slabs, along which there is a fork by a low wooden post. The laid path continues to the left, but you need to bear right on to a not-so-well-defined path, which soon swings round and heads directly towards the gap in the wall, to the right of which is a ladder stile. Climb the ladder stile, then continue along the path that heads through the middle of the shallow saddle ahead.

You are now following the line of the Lleyn Coastal Path, and although the path varies between indistinct and fairly good, at least there are laid stone slabs across the boggiest sections. Two lesser paths (the first of which is waymarked) veer off to the left, heading towards the obvious rocky knoll of Caergribin, another fine viewpoint, but the main route continues through the saddle to reach a metal kissing gate. There is nothing to prevent you from visiting Caergribin if you so wish – if you do so, make your way back to the coastal path by any of several indistinct paths, and thus to the kissing gate.

Beyond the kissing gate, the route of the coastal path is obvious, heading slightly downhill into the valley ahead. Ignore this, instead bearing off to the right, following a path that traverses the hillside, keeping as near as possible to the same level at all junctions. Eventually, close to where the path approaches the top of the ridge ahead, you should be able to make out the tops of the conifers adjacent to the car park. At this point you should bear right across easy ground, heading first towards the trees, then down to meet the track along which you travelled on your outward route, from where it is a simple matter to retrace your steps to the start. Alternatively, in misty conditions, keep following the level path until you reach a long, stone wall, and turn right alongside the wall to reach the same point.

# SELECT BIBLIOGRAPHY

While a considerable amount of research for this book was done by asking local people and then using the internet and the local library to substantiate or expand on their stories, the following books were particularly useful.

Bick, David, *The Old Metal Mines of Mid Wales (Vols 4 & 5)* (The Pound House, 1990).

Bick, David, *The Old Copper Mines of Snowdonia* (Landmark Publishing, 2003).

Brown, Michael, *Dylife* (Dinas, 2005).

Godwin, Fay, & Toulson, Shirley, *The Drovers' Roads of Wales* (Whittet Books, 1977).

Lewis, M.J.T., & Denton, J.H., *Rhosydd Slate Quarry* (The Cottage Press, 1974).

*Walks and Rides along the Brinore Tramroad* (The Brinore Conservation Forum, 2003).

*Welsh Gold: The Story of Gwynfynydd* (Aur Cymru Ccc).